Originally published by Politikens Forlag, Vestergade 26, 1456 København K

First published in Great Britain in 2025 by Ilex, a division of Octopus Publishing Group Ltd, Carmelite House, 50 Victoria Embankment, London, EC4Y 0DZ
www.octopusbooks.co.uk
www.octopusbooksusa.com

An Hachette UK Company
www.hachette.co.uk

The authorized representative in the EEA is Hachette Ireland, 8 Castlecourt Centre, Dublin 15, D15 XTP3, Ireland (email: info@hbgi.ie)

Distributed in the US by
Hachette Book Group
1290 Avenue of the Americas,
4th & 5th Floors, New York, NY 10104

Distributed in Canada by
Canadian Manda Group
664 Annette Street, Toronto,
Ontario MS62C8

ISBN 978-1-84091-906-6

A CIP catalogue record for this book is available from the British Library
Printed and bound in China

10 9 8 7 6 5 4 3 2 1

For Ilex:
Publisher: Alison Starling
Commissioning Editor: Ellie Corbett
Managing Editor: Rachel Silverlight
Translation from Danish: Robin Orm Hansen
Art Director: Ben Gardiner
Typesetting: Jeremy Tilston
Production Managers:
Lucy Carter and Nic Jones

Modern Danish Knitting

From cult pattern makers
SPEKTAKELSTRIK

Mie Firring

Contents

Foreword → 6
Let's Get Started! → 8

Erika Jumper → 12
Erika Dress → 16
Erika Slipover → 24
Mega Erika Jumper → 28
Decadent Sweater → 36
Decadent Dress → 42
Lykke Jumper → 46
Bibi Sweater → 48
Mega Bibi Slipover → 54
Bibi Scarf → 60
Stripe Overload for Sighthounds → 64
Stripe Overload for Most Dogs → 67
Fat Fur Sweater for Sighthounds → 70
Fat Fur Sweater for Most Dogs → 73
Stripe Overload Polo → 76

Hilda Oversize Slipover → 80
Hilda Sweater → 84
Icelandic Hilda → 88
Mohairy Sweater → 92
Crew Sweater → 98
Crew Skirt → 102
Oversize Crew Sweater → 104
Crew Pants → 110
Waves Sweater → 114
Bianca Slipover → 118
Fat Fur Hat → 126
Fat Fur Boa → 128
Rose Sweater → 130
Lace Polo → 134

Yarns → 140
Abbreviations → 142
Thanks! → 144

Foreword

I am quite impulsive, and for me, it's never been far from idea to creation. I love to make something by hand. When I get a good idea, I can feel it, deep in my body. It sifts through my whole being and it becomes the only thing I focus on.

I always start with a clear idea, and then I draft it out. And I can quickly sense whether the idea will work. If it demonstrates that it won't work out, the spark disappears, and I have to take a different route.

I prefer to do something I haven't thought through, just to try it out. That means that I've often had to rip out my knitting – really often. But that's completely okay, because that's part of the process. The work is never wasted, because ideas have to be tested.

If the idea is good, I have a head start – and then, it's hard to put down the idea or even the process until I have a finished product.

From the very beginning, my idea with this book has been to work with repeats. To knit is to repeat. It's the same movement over and over and over. The one stitch after the other. To knit is also to repeat in the sense of carrying a tradition forward, from the generations before us and to those who will follow us.

There's comfort in repeating. It keeps my hands occupied and calms my mind. I'm dependent on repetition. Get up, go to work, shop, come home, make supper. The repetition and everyday predictability means I can provide for myself and unfold myself artistically. It means that I can thrive at being an initiator, make choices without thinking them through and go with my gut feeling.

We also see repetition in mass production. Furniture and objects can be repeated into eternity. The white plastic deck chair. The wine glass in transparent plastic. Artificial turf. I find this enormously fascinating.

What happens when we place production and handcraft repetitions side by side? This is the question I've chosen to explore in this book's visual concept. Because repetition is important – in both everyday life and in a knitting pattern.

I work visually, and this characterizes my book. You won't find long, vivid descriptions for each pattern, because text is not my medium. So, there isn't much irrelevant chatter. Rather, I've gone to some trouble to write the directions to be easily understood and just right to jump into.

Let's get started!

When you read through a pattern's directions, they may seem a little overwhelming. As I said earlier, the energy lies in my hands. And sometimes, it can be easier to understand the directions with *your* hands. If something looks difficult, don't worry about it. Just begin. There's a good chance that the whole thing will make sense when you start knitting.

Have fun!

Mie Firring Christiansen

Let's Get Started!

Knitting Gauge/Tension and Swatches
Making a test swatch is alpha and omega. You may really want to just launch into knitting right off. But without a test swatch, you won't know whether your knitting gauge/tension will match the measurements in the pattern, so then, you can't be sure that your finished product will be the right size and shape.

All the patterns show the knitting tension as the number of stitches and rows in a 10cm (4in) square.

For example, in the *Faux-Fur Hat* (p. 126): 12 sts and 18 rows on 6mm (US 10) [UK 4] needles = 10 × 10cm (4 × 4in) square in stockinette with 2 strands. This means, that when you knit 12 sts with 2 strands of yarn in stockinette for 18 rows on size 6mm (US 10) [UK 4] needles you should arrive at a square patch measuring 10 × 10cm (4 × 4in).

However, it's a good idea to cast on more sts than suggested when making your tension swatch. That will make it easier to measure the finished swatch. If you want to be completely sure of measuring correctly, you can, for example, cast on 10 more stitches and knit some extra rows. In the *Faux-Fur Hat* example, that would mean that I might cast on a total 22 sts and knit, perhaps, 24 rows.

Before measuring your tension swatch, it should be washed and dried, which you will also do with your finished project. If your test swatch then measures less than given in the pattern, you should try again with a larger size needle. If your test swatch is bigger than the pattern calls for, try a smaller size needle. It's all about trying things out until you've found the right size knitting needles that hit the correct knitting tension.

Knitting Needles
I always use circular needles for my knitting and the 'Magic Loop' technique. If you do so too, you will need only one kind of needle for both long and short rounds. If you don't want to use Magic Loop, you can substitute double-pointed needles for short rounds.

Abbreviations
All abbreviations are listed and explained at the end of this book. See p. 142.

Video Guides
On Spektakelstrik.dk you will find links to videos that guide you through the techniques used in this book.

Alternative Yarns
If you want to use a different yarn than suggested in the directions, it is important that the yarn can be worked at the given knitting tension and has the same meterage/yardage per the weight of ball given as the yarn in the directions. For yardage and ounces per skein, see page 140. Remember to make a tension swatch and measure it afterwards.

Assembly
Generally speaking, all the patterns in this book are worked in one piece. That means that they either need minimal assembly or are completely free of assembly work.

Washing and Blocking
Before you use your knitted project, it should be washed and possibly blocked so that the fibres bloom and settle into place. Always follow the washing and blocking directions on the yarn's label.

Carefully squeeze the water out of your project before letting it dry. NEVER wring it out, as you may risk pulling it out of shape.

Then I always give it a gentle whirl in the spin cycle of my washing machine. *NOTE:* Take care: Spinning is up to you, as washing machines differ. If you want to be completely sure of not felting your knitwear, lay it out to dry as described below.

Finally, I spread my project out and lay it out to dry on, for example, a towel. It can be spread on a floor with working radiant heat. The most important thing is to lay it out on a flat surface.

Some knitting also requires blocking, for example, knitting with a lace or lattice pattern. In such cases, I lay it out on a piece of foam after washing, then pin it into shape. Then, I know it will have the desired shape. It can be a good idea to buy a blocking kit with T-pins for this purpose.

EDITION

A top in lattice-knitting, fastened with i-cord ties

Erika Jumper

Sizes
XS (S) M (L) XL (XXL)

Measurements
Chest: 92 (99) 106 (114) 116 (127)cm
[36.25 (39) 41.75 (45) 45.75 (46)in]
Length: 46 (48) 49 (51) 52 (52)cm
[18 (19) 19.25 (20) 20.5 (20.5)in]
Sleeve length: 42 (42) 42 (41) 41 (41)cm
[16.5 (16.5) 16.5 (16) 16 (16)in]

Needles
Circular needle, 3.5mm (US 4)
[UK 9 or 10], 80cm [32in]
Tapestry needle for finishing.

Knitting Gauge/Tension
17 sts x 27 rows in pattern on 3.5mm (US 4)
[UK 9 or 10] needles = 10 × 10cm (4 × 4in)

The pattern is a multiple of 3
including 2 selvage stitches.

Yarns
Gepardgarn's Cotton Wool 5
Colour 832 (green):
450 (500) 550 (600) 650 (700)g

Info
The topper is knitted from the top down. The top of the front is worked first and the back pieces are picked up from the shoulders of the front and all are worked together from the underarm down. Later, stitches are picked up for the sleeves and neck band.

The lattice-stitch pattern is unusual and tricky, but once you have it in hand, it flows. Master it while making your test swatch.

The square hole of lattice stitch is a multiple of 4 rows and 3 sts, including a first st and 2 final (total 3) selvage stitches.

A selvage- or edge-stitch is worked by slipping the first st p-wise with the yarn in front of the needle. In the next row, from the wrong side, the same st is knitted.

The holes are separated vertically by 2 knit rows:
Row 1 (ws). K to end of row.
Row 2 (rs). K to end of row.
Row 3 (ws). Knit 1, purl 2 together, yarn over (yo), yarn over, *then, purl a centred double decrease (p ctr dbl dec): Slip 2 sts, one by one, as if to knit, insert left needle in next-to-last st on right needle from front and slip both it and last st together onto left needle. Purl 3 together (those 2 sts and the next st), yarn over, yarn over. Rep from * until 2 sts remain. Knit 2.
Row 4 (rs). K1, *k2, p1. Rep from * to end of row. The 2nd knit st is worked into the first yarn-over from the previous row. The purl st is worked in the second yarn over. This seems unlikely but works neatly and easily.

Front Right Shoulder
Cast on 27 (30) 33 (36) 39 (42) sts on 3.5mm (US 4) [UK 9 or 10] circular needle.

Knit straight down in lattice pattern, starting on the wrong side:
Row 1 (ws). K to end of row.
Row 2 (rs). K to end of row.
Row 3. K1, p2tog, yo, yo, k1, p2tog, yo, yo, *p ctr dbl dec, yo, yo.
Rep from * until 3 sts remain, p2tog through back, k1.
Row 4. K1, *k2, p1. Rep from * until 2 sts remain, k2.

Work Rows 1-4 a total 6 (6) 6 (6) 7 (7) times.

Now inc to shape left edge of neckline.
Work 8 rows, increasing in Rows 4, 5, 6, and 8 only:
Rows 1 (ws). K to end of row.
Row 2 (rs). K to end of row.
Row 3. K1, p2tog, yo, yo, *p ctr dbl dec, yo, yo.
Rep from * until 3 sts remain, p2tog through back, k1 .
Row 4. (Inc) K1, *k2, p1. Rep from * until 2 sts remain, k1, make 1 rt, k1.
Row 5. (Inc) K1, make 1 left, k to end of row.
Row 6. (Inc) Knit until 1 st remains, make 1 rt, k1.
Row 7. K1, p2tog, yo, yo, *p ctr dbl dec, yo, yo. Rep from * until 3 sts remain,

p2tog through back loop, k1.
Row 8. (Inc) K1, *k2, p1. Rep from *
until 2 sts remain, k1, make 1 rt, k1.
Total 31 (34) 37 (40) 43 (46) sts.
Break yarn and place sts on a holder.

Front Left Shoulder
Cast on 27 (30) 33 (36) 39 (42) sts on 3.5mm (US 4) [UK 9 or 10] needles.
K4 rows.
Work even in lattice pattern:
Rows 1 (ws) and **2 (rs).** K to end of row.
Row 3. K1, p2tog, yo, yo,
*p ctr dbl dec, yo, yo.
Rep from * until 3 sts remain,
tw p2tog, k1.
Row 4. K1, *k2, p1. Rep from *
until 2 sts remain, k2.

Work Rows 1–4 a total 6 (6) 6 (6) 7 (7) times. (Count rows of holes to measure.)

Now inc to shape the right edge of the neckline.
Work these 8 rows:
Row 1 (ws). K to end of row.
Row 2 (rs). K to end of row.
Row 3 (ws). K1, p2tog, yo, yo,
*p ctr dbl dec, yo, yo. Rep from * until 3 sts remain, p2tog through back loop, k1.
Row 4 (rs). K1, make 1 left, *k2, p1.
Rep from * until 2 sts remain, k2.
Row 5 (ws). K even until 1 st remains, make 1 rt, k1.
Row 6 (rs). K1, make 1 left, k to end of row.
Row 7 (ws). K1, p2tog, yo, yo,
*p ctr dbl dec, yo, yo.
Rep from * until 3 sts remain, tw p2tog, k1.
Row 8 (rs). K1, make 1 left, *k2, p1.
Rep from * until 2 sts remain, k2.
Total 31 (34) 37 (40) 43 (46) sts.

Now join the 2 front shoulder pieces, starting on wrong side:
Next row. K even until 1 st remains, make 1 left, k1, cast on 11 neckline sts, place right shoulder sts on the needle, neck-edges facing, and k to end of row.
Total 75 (81) 87 (93) 99 (105) sts.

Next row (rs). K to end of row.
Next row (ws). (Lattice pattern) K1, p2tog, yo, yo, *p ctr dbl dec, yo, yo.
Rep from * until 3 sts remain, tw p2tog, k1.
Next row (rs). K1, *k2, p1. Rep from *
until 2 sts remain, k2.

Now work even in lattice pattern:
Rows 1 (ws) and 2 (rs). K to end of row.
Row 3 (ws). K1, p2tog, yo, yo,
*p ctr dbl dec, yo, yo. Rep from *
until 3 sts remain, tw p2tog, k1.
Row 4. K1, *k2, p1. Rep from *
until 2 sts remain, k2.
Work Rows 1–4 until front measures 20 (21) 22 (23) 24 (25)cm
[8 (8.25) 8.6 (9) 9.5 (9.8)in].
End with Row 1.
Break yarn and place sts on a holder.

Back Right Shoulder
Pick up and knit 27 (30) 33 (36) 39 (42) sts from the right front shoulder from the right side on 3.5mm (US 4) [UK 9 or 10] needles.
K4 rows.
Now work these 4 rows:
Row 1 (ws). K1, p2tog, yo, yo,
*p ctr dob dec, yo, yo.
Rep from * until 3 sts remain, tw p2tog, k1.
Row 2. K1, *k2, p1. Rep from *
until 2 sts remain, k2.
Row 3. K to end of row, then shape neckline: Cast on 11 sts.
Row 4. K to end of row.
Total 38 (41) 44 (47) 50 (53) sts.

Knit even in lattice pattern:
Row 1 (ws). K1, p2tog, yo, yo,
*p ctr dbl dec, yo, yo.
Rep from *until 5 sts remain,
p2tog through back loop, k3.
Row 2. Sl 1 p-wise, k2, *k2 , p1. Rep from *
until 2 sts remain, k2.
Row 3. K to end of row.
Row 4. Sl 1 p-wise, k to end of row.

Rep Rows 1–4 until the back has 1 fewer rows of holes than the front. End with Row 2.
Break yarn and place sts on a holder.

Back Left Shoulder
Pick up 27 (30) 33 (36) 39 (42) sts up from the outside of the right front shoulder 3.5mm (US 4) [UK 9 or 10] needles. K4 rows.

Now, work these 4 rows:
Row 1 (ws). K1, p2tog, yo, yo, *p ctr dbl dec, yo, yo. Rep from * until 3 sts remain, tw p2tog. k1.
Row 2 (rs). K1, *k2, p1. Rep from
* until 2 sts remain, K2.
Then cast on 11 sts for neckline.
Row 3 (ws). K to end of row.

Row 4 (rs). K to end of row.
Total 38 (41) 44 (47) 50 (53) sts.

Work even in lattice pattern:
Row 1 (ws). Sl 1 p-wise, k2, p2tog, yo, yo, *p ctr dbl dec, yo, yo.
Rep from * until 3 sts remain, tw p2tog, k1.
Row 2 (rs). K1, *k2, p1. Rep from * until 4 sts remain, k4.
Row 3 (ws). Sl 1 p-wise, k to end of row.
Row 4 (rs). K to end of row.
Rep Rows 1–4 until the back has one fewer rows of holes than the front.
End with Row 2.

Body
Join the front and back panels, starting on ws with the back left shoulder piece: Sl 1 p-wise, k the sts on the needle, cast on 3 sts for left underarm, put the front sts on the needle with wrong sides matching, k the front sts, cast on 3 sts for right underarm, put the right back shoulder sts on the needle and knit to end of row.

Next Row (rs). Sl 1 p-wise, k to end of row.
Total 157 (169) 181 (193) 205 (217) sts.

Now continue even in lattice pattern:
Row 1 (ws). Sl 1 p-wise, k2, p2tog, yo, yo, *p ctr dbl dec, yo, yo.
Rep from * until 5 sts remain, K2tog through back loop, k3.
Row 2 (rs). Sl 1 p-wise, k2, *k2, p1. Rep from * until 4 sts remain, k4.
Row 3 (ws). Sl 1 p-wise, k to end of row.
Row 4 (rs). Sl 1 p-wise, k to end of row.

Rep Rows 1–4 until the whole piece from the top of the shoulder down measures 45 (46) 47 (48) 49 (50)cm [17.75 (18) 18.5 (19) 19.25 (19.75)in].
End with Row 2.

Next 4 rows. Sl 1 p-wise, k to end of row.
Now, bind off in knit on the wrong side.

Sleeves
The two sleeves are identical. Start at the centre of the underarm on rs.
Pick up and knit 66 (69) 72 (78) 81 (84) sts around the armhole from the rs.
(pick up approx 2 to 3 sts per hole in in the lattice). It is important that total number of sts is divisible by 3.

Continue to end of rnd and place st marker. Knit 1 rnd (ws).

Now work around in lattice pattern:
Rnd 1 (ws). *Ctr dbl dec, yo, yo.
Rep from * to marker at beg of rnd.
Rnd 2. *K2, p1. Rep from * to end of rnd.
Rnd 3 (ws). P to end of rnd.
Rnd 4. K until 1 st remains. Sl the last st onto the right needle without knitting it, remove st marker and replace the st on the left needle and place the marker on the rt needle again. You are moving the beg of the rnd 1 st to the right.

Rep Rnds 1–4 until the sleeve measures 41 (41) 41 (40) 40 (40) cm [16.25 (16.25) 16.25 (15.75) 15.75 (15.75)in]. End with Rnd 2.

K 1 rnd, p 1 rnd, k 1 rnd, p 1 rnd, k 1 rnd, turn work around (you can make a short row turn st here if desired).
Bind off in knit on the wrong side.

Neck
Start on the left back neck edge.
(Do not change needle size.)
Pick up and k approx 98 (98) 98 (98) 98 (98) sts along the neck opening working on the outside.

Next 4 rows. Sl 1 p-wise, k to end of row.

Bind off in knit on the ws.

Ties
You will make 6 ties altogether.
Working on rs, pick up 3 sts at the top of the neckline in back in the outermost 3 sts and knit i-cord:
K3 sts, *Staying on rs, slip the 3 sts back to the left needle, and k3. Rep from * until the tie measures 34cm [13.5in], stretched taut. Bind off.
Knit 5 more ties the same way: one opposite the first tie; 2 ties $1/3$ of the total length farther down, and finally 2 ties $2/3$ down from the top (See illustration, p 12.)

Finishing
You're all done: All parts are already assembled.
Work all loose ends into sts on ws.

A sleeveless gown in lattice stitch, closed in back with i-cord ties

Erika Dress

Sizes
XS (S) M (L) XL (XXL)

Measurements
Chest: 94 (101) 108 (115) 118 (129)cm
37 (39.75) 42.5 (45.25) 46.5 (50.75)in]
Full length: 109 (110) 111 (112) 113 (114)cm
[43 (43.25) 43.75 (44) 44.5 (45)in]

Needles
Circular needle 3mm (US 2.5)
[UK 11], 60cm [24in]
Circular needle 3.5mm (US 4)
[UK 9 or 10], 80cm [32in]
Tapestry needle for finishing.

Knitting Gauge/Tension
17 sts x 27 rows in pattern on 3.5mm (US 4) [UK 9 or 10] needles = 10 × 10cm (4 × 4in)

The lattice pattern is divisible by 3, including 2 selvage stitches.

Yarn
Gepardgarn's Cotton Wool 5
Colour 531 (light blue):
550 (600) 650 (700) 750 (800)g

Info
The gown is knitted from the top down. The back shoulders and armholes are made first, the front is picked up from the back shoulders, all three pieces are joined at the underarm and when knitting reaches the bottom of the back opening, the garment is knitted circularly until the 30cm [12in] slit in the right side. The bottom is then knitted back and forth, maintaining the boxy grid appearance throughout. Last of all, sts are picked up to i-cord finish the neckline and to make the ties in back.

The lattice-stitch pattern is unusual and tricky, but once you have it in hand, it flows. Master it while making your test swatch.

The square hole of lattice stitch is a multiple of 4 rows and 3 sts, including a 1st and 2 final (total 3) selvage stitches.

A selvage- or edge-stitch is worked by slipping the first st purlwise with the yarn in front of the needle. In the next row, from the wrong side, the same st is knitted.

All odd-numbered rows here are on wrong side/purl side (ws).
All even-numbered rows are on right/knit side (rs). You can tell whether you're on an odd or an even numbered row by the location of your cast-on tail.
On odd rows (ws), the tail is on your right.

Start with 2 knit rows for garter st.

Row 1 (ws). K to end of row.
Row 2 (rs). K to end of row.
Row 3 (ws). Knit 1, purl 2 together, yarn over (yo), yarn over, *purl a centred double decrease (p ctr dbl dec): Slip 2 sts, one by one, as if to knit, insert left needle in next-to-last st on right needle from front and slip both it and last st together onto left needle. Purl 3 together (those 2 sts and the next st), yarn over, yarn over.
Rep from * until 2 sts remain, k2.
Row 4 (rs). K1, *k2, p1. Rep from * to end of row. The 2nd knit st is worked into the first yarn-over from the previous row. The purl st is worked in the second yarn over. This seems unlikely but works neatly and easily.

Right Back Panel
Cast on 17 (17) 20 (20) 23 (23) sts on 3.5mm (US 4) [UK 9 or 10] needles.

Work these 8 rows:
Row 1 (ws). Sl 1 p-wise, k to end of row.
Row 2 (rs). K to end of row.
Row 3. Sl 1 p-wise, k to end of row.
Row 4. K to end of row.
Row 5. Sl 1 p-wise, k2, p2tog, yo, yo, *p ctr dbl dec, yo, yo. Rep from * until 3 sts remain, k2tog through back loop, k1.
Row 6. K1, *k2, p1. Rep from * until 4 sts remain, k4 .
Row 7. Sl 1 p-wise, k to end of row and cast on 11 sts for neckline.
Row 8. Sl 1 p-wise, k to end of row.
Total: 28 (28) 31 (31) 34 (34) sts.

Continue even in lattice st:
Row 1 (ws). Sl 1 p-wise, k2, p2tog, yo, yo, *p ctr dbl dec, yo, yo. Rep from * until 5 sts remain, p2tog through back loop, k3.
Row 2 (rs). Sl 1 p-wise, k2, *k2, p1.* Rep from * until 4 sts remain, k4.
Row 3. Sl 1 p-wise, k to end of row.
Row 4. Sl 1 p-wise, k to end of row.

Work Rows 1–4 a total of 8 (8) 8 (8) 9 (9) times. (It's easier to count rows of holes than actual knit rows in this pattern.) Work Rows 1–2 again.

Now work 4 rows and inc on Row 4 on the side toward the armhole:
Row 1 (ws). Sl 1 p-wise, k to end of row.
Row 2 (rs). Sl 1 p-wise, k to end of row.
Row 3. Sl 1 p-wise, K2, p2tog, yo, yo, *p ctr dbl dec, yo, yo. Rep from * until 5 sts remain, tw p2tog, k3.
Row 4. Sl 1 p-wise, k2, *k2, p1. Rep from * until 4 sts remain, k1, inc 1 rt, k3. Total 29 (29) 32 (32) 35 (35) sts.

Now inc:
Row 1 (ws). Sl 1 p-wise, k2, make 1 left, k until 3 sts remain, k3.
Row 2 (rs). Sl 1 p-wise, k2, k until 3 sts remain, make 1 rt, k3.
Row 3. Sl 1 p-wise, k2, p2tog, yo, yo, *p ctr dbl dec, yo, yo. Rep from * until 5 sts remain, p2tog through back loop, k3.
Row 4. Sl 1 p-wise, k2, *k2, p1. Rep from * until 4 sts remain, k1, make 1 rt, k3.

Work Rows 1–4 a total 2 (3) 3 (4) 4 (5) times = 35 (38) 41 (44) 47 (50) sts.

Now inc:
Row 1 (ws). Sl 1 k-wise, k2, make 1 left, k until 3 sts remain, k3.
Row 2. Sl 1 p-wise, k2, k until 3 sts remain, make 1 rt, k3.
Row 3. Sl 1 p-wise, k2, p2tog, yo, yo, *p ctr dbl dec, yo, yo. Rep from * until 5 sts remain, tw p2tog, k3.
Row 4. Sl 1 p-wise, k2 *k2, p1*. Rep from * until 4 sts remain, k4. Total 37 (40) 43 (46) 49 (52) sts.

From this point, work even in lattice st until the piece measures 19 (20) 21 (22) 23 (24)cm [7.5 (8) 8.25 (8.5) 9 (9.5) in] at the longest point. End with Row 4. Break yarn and place sts on a holder.

Right Front Shoulder
With 3.5mm (US 4) [UK 9 or 10] needles, pick up and knit 17 (17) 20 (20) 23 (23) sts from the rs at the top of the back right shoulder.

Work even in lattice st:
Row 1 (ws). K to end of row.
Row 2 (rs). Sl 1 p-wise, k to end of row.
Row 3. K1, p2tog, yo, yo, *p ctr dbl dec, yo, yo. Rep from * until 5 sts remain, p2tog through back loop, k3.
Row 4. Sl 1 p-wise, k2 *k2, p1. Rep from* until 2 sts remain, k2.

Work Rows 1–4 a total of 6 (6) 6 (6) 7 (7) times.

Now inc to shape the neckline on the front left side of work. Work 8 rows:
Row 1 (ws). K to end of row.
Row 2 (rs). Sl 1 p-wise, k to end of row.
Row 3. K1, p2tog, yo, yo, *p ctr dbl dec, yo, yo. Rep from * until 5 sts remain, p2tog through back loop, k3.
Row 4. (Inc) Sl 1 p-wise, k2 *k2, p1. Rep from * until 2 sts remain, k1, make 1 rt, k1.
Row 5. (Inc) K1, make 1 left, k to end of row.
Row 6. (Inc) Sl 1 p-wise, k until 1 st remains, make 1 rt, k1.
Row 7. K1, p2tog, yo, yo,*p ctr dbl dec, yo, yo. Rep from * until 3 sts remain, tw p2tog, k1, k1.
Row 8. (Inc) Sl 1 p-wise, k2, k2, p1. Rep from * until 2 sts remain, k1, make 1 rt, k1.
Total 21 (21) 24 (24) 27 (27) sts.
Break yarn and place sts on a holder.

Left Back Shoulder
Cast on 17 (17) 20 (20) 23 (23) sts on 3.5mm (US 4) [UK 9 or 10] needles.

Work 8 rows:
Starting on ws, k4 rows, slipping 1 st p-wise at beg of each rs row.
Row 5 (ws). K1, p2tog, yo, yo, *p ctr dbl dec, yo, yo. Rep from * until 5 sts remain, tw p2 sts tog, k3.
Row 6 (rs). Sl 1 p-wise, k2, *k2, p1. Rep from * until 2 sts remain, k2. Cast on 11 sts.
Row 7 (ws) and Row 8 (rs). Sl 1 p-wise, k to end of row.
Total 28 (28) 31 (31) 34 (34) sts.

Work even in lattice st for armhole:
Row 1 (ws). Sl 1 p-wise, k2, p2tog, yo, yo, *p ctr dbl dec, yo, yo. Rep from * until 5 sts remain, tw p2tog, k3.

Row 2 (rs). Sl 1 p-wise, k2, *k2, p1. Rep from * until 4 sts remain, k4.
Row 3 (ws). Sl 1 p-wise, k to end of row.
Row 4 (rs). Sl 1 p-wise, k to end of row.

Work Rows 1–4 a total 8 (8) 8 (8) 9 (9) times.
Work Rows 1–2 again.

Now work 4 rows and inc on Row 4 to shape the underarm:
Rows 1 (ws) and 2 (rs). Sl 1 p-wise, k to end of row.
Row 3 (ws). Sl 1 p-wise, k2, p2tog, yo, yo, *p ctr dbl dec, yo, yo. Rep from * until 5 sts remain, tw p2tog, k3.
Row 4. (Inc) Sl 1 p-wise, k2, make 1 left, *k2, p1. Rep from*, until 4 sts remain, k4.
Total 29 (29) 32 (32) 35 (35) sts.

Now increase:
Row 1 (ws). (Inc) Sl 1 p-wise, k until 3 sts remain, make 1 rt, k3.
Row 2 (rs). (Inc) Sl 1 p-wise, k2, make 1 left, k to end of row.
Row 3 (ws). Sl 1 p-wise, k2, p2tog, yo, yo, *p ctr dbl dec, yo, yo. Rep from * until 5 sts remain, tw p2tog, k3.
Row 4 (rs). (Inc) Sl 1 p-wise, k2, make 1 left, *k2, p1. Rep from * until 4 sts remain, k4.

Work Rows 1–4 a total 2 (3) 3 (4) 4 (5) times = 35 (38) 41 (44) 47 (50) sts.

Now increase:
Row 1 (ws). (Inc) Sl 1 p-wise, k until 3 sts remain , make 1 rt, k3.
Row 2 (rs). (Inc) Sl 1 p-wise, k2, make 1 left, k to end of row.
Row 3 (ws). Sl 1 p-wise, k2, p2tog, yo, yo, *p ctr dbl dec, yo, yo. Rep from * until 5 sts remain. tw p2tog, k3.
Row 4 (rs). Sl 1 p-wise, k2, *k2, p1. Rep from * until 4 sts remain, k4.
Total 37 (40) 43 (46) 49 (52) sts.

From here on, knit even (no incs) in lattice st until piece measures 19 (20) 21 (22) 23 (24)cm [7.5 (7.75) 8.25 (8.75) 9 (9.5)in] .
End with Row 4.
Break yarn and place sts on a holder.

Left Front Shoulder
With 3.5mm (US 4) [UK 9 or 10] needles, working from the rs, pick up and knit 17 (17) 20 (20) 23 (23) sts from the top of the back left shoulder.

Work even (no incs) in lattice st:
Row 1 (ws). Sl 1 p-wise, k to end of row.
Row 2 (rs). K to end of row.
Row 3. Sl 1 p-wise, k2, p2tog, yo, yo, *p ctr dbl dec, yo, yo. Rep from * until 3 sts remain, tw p2tog, k1.
Row 4. K1 *k2, p1. Rep from * until 4 sts remain, k4.

Rep these 4 rows 6 (6) 6 (6) 7 (7) times.

Now inc to form the neckline to the rt.
Work 8 rows with incs on Rows 4, 5, 6, and 8:
Row 1 (ws). Sl 1 p-wise, k to end of rnd.
Row 2 (rs). K to end of row.
Row 3. Sl 1 p-wise, k2, p2tog, yo, yo, *p ctr dbl dec, yo, yo. Rep from * until 3 sts remain, tw p2tog, k1.
Row 4. (Inc) K1, make 1 left, *k2, p1. Rep from * until 4 sts remain, k4.
Row 5. (Inc) Sl 1 p-wise, k until 1 st remains, make 1 rt, k1.
Row 6. (Inc) K1, make 1 left, k to end of row.
Row 7. Sl 1 p-wise, k2, p2tog, yo, yo, *p ctr dbl dec, yo, yo. Rep from * until 3 sts remain, tw p2tog, k1.
Row 8. (Inc) K1, make 1 left, *k2, p1. Rep from * until 4 sts remain, k4.
Total 21 (21) 24 (24) 27 (27) sts.

Join the 2 front shoulder pieces:
Next row (ws). Sl 1 p-wise, k until 1 st remains on needle, k1, cast on 11 sts (all sizes), replace the right front shoulder sts on the left needle, matching ws together, k1, make 1 left, k remaining sts.
Total 55 (55) 61 (61) 67 (67) sts.

Next row (rs). Sl 1 p-wise, k to end of row.
Next row (ws). Sl 1 p-wise, k2, p2tog, yo, yo, *p ctr dbl dec, yo, yo. Rep from * until 5 sts remain, tw p2tog, k3.
Next row (rs). Sl 1 p-wise, k2, *k2, p1. Rep from * until 4 sts remain, k4.

Now inc for underarms on both sides of the linked front shoulder pieces. Work these 4 rows, with incs in Row 4:
Row 1 (ws). Sl 1 p-wise, k to end of row.
Row 2 (rs). Sl 1 p-wise, k to end of row.
Row 3. Sl 1 p-wise, k2, p2tog, yo, yo. *p ctr dbl dec, yo, yo. Rep from * until 5 sts remain, tw p2tog, k3.
Row 4. (Inc) Sl 1 p-wise, k2, make

1 left, *k2, p1. Rep from * until 4 sts remain, k1, make 1 rt, k3. Total 57 (57) 63 (63) 69 (69) sts.

Now inc in all but Row 3:
Row 1 (ws). (Inc) Sl 1 p-wise, k2, make 1 left, k until 3 sts remain, make 1 rt, k3.
Row 2 (rs). (Inc) Sl 1 p-wise, k2, make 1 left, k until 3 sts remain, make 1 rt, k3.
Row 3. Sl 1 p-wise, k2, p2tog, yo, yo, *p ctr dbl dec, yo, yo. Rep from * until 5 sts remain, tw p2tog, k3.
Row 4. (Inc) Sl 1 p-wise, k2, make 1 left, *K2, p1. Rep from * until 4 sts remain, k1, make 1 rt, k3.

Work Rows 1–4 a total 2 (3) 3 (4) 4 (5) times = 69 (75) 81 (87) 93 (99) sts.

Knit these 6 rows with increases on Rows 1–2:
Row 1 (ws). (Inc) Sl 1 p-wise, k2, make 1 left, k until 3 sts remain in row, make 1 rt, k3.
Row 2 (rs). (Inc) Sl 1 p-wise, k2, make 1 left, k to 3 sts remain, make 1 rt, k3.
Row 3 (ws). Sl 1 p-wise, k2, p2tog, yo, yo, *p ctr dbl dec, yo, yo. Rep from * until 5 sts remain, tw p2tog, k3.
Row 4. Sl 1 p-wise, *k2, p1. Rep from * until 4 sts remain, k4.
Rows 5 and 6. Sl 1 p-wise, k to end of row.
Total 73 (79) 85 (91) 97 (103) sts .

Work even in lattice st, always starting with sl 1 purl-wise and ending Row 1 with k3, 2nd rows with k4.

Rep Rows 1–4 until the front is as long as the back piece. End with Row 2 of lattice st. Break yarn and place sts on a holder.

Join front and back pieces at the underarm: Working from ws, place left back shoulder sts onto 3.5mm (US 4) [UK 9 or 10] needles, Sl 1 p-wise and knit to end of row.

Cast on 5 sts for left underarm, place the front piece sts back on the needle, matching right and wrong sides and knit to end of row.

Cast on 5 sts for right underarm, put right back shoulder sts on needle and k to end of row.

Next row (rs). Sl 1 p-wise, k to end of row.
Total 157 (169) 181 (193) 205 (217) sts.
Now work even in lattice st:
Row 1 (ws). Sl 1 p-wise, k1, p2tog, yo, yo; *p ctr dbl dec, yo, yo. Rep from * until 5 sts remain, tw p2tog, k3.
Row 2 (rs). Sl 1 p-wise, k2, *k2, p1. Rep from * until 4 sts remain, k4.
Row 3. Sl 1 p-wise, k to end of row.
Row 4. Sl 1 p-wise, k to end of row.

Rep Rows 1–4 until the back opening measures 26 (27) 27 (28) 28 (28)cm [10.25 (10.75) 10.75 (11) 11 (11)in]. End with Row 3.

Break yarn and move the first 37 (40) 43 (46) 49 (52) sts of the next row onto the right needle. Place st marker for beg of new rnd and attach yarn to work from that point.

Work full row of knit (Row 4 of st pattern) until 3 sts remain in the row, place st marker (to mark point of later side slit in skirt) and cast on 2 sts, k remaining 3 sts, and k the sts of the left back panel up to rnd marker.

You will now work circularly from the right side only, instead of back and forth.

Body
Rnd 1. *Ctr dbl dec, yo, yo. Rep from * until 2 sts before marker for side slit, k2tog, p8, tw k2tog, yo, yo. Rep from * to end of rnd.
Rnd 2. *K2, p1. Rep from * to 1 st before the placket marker, k9, then *k2, p1. Rep from * to complete the rnd.
Rnd 3. P to end of rnd.
Rnd 4. K to 1 st before rnd marker, slip that st onto right needle without knitting it, remove the marker, place the slipped st back on the left needle and replace the marker, so that the start of the rnd has moved 1 st to the right.

Rep Rnds 1–4 once.
Total 159 (171) 183 (195) 207 (219) sts.

Now work even in the 4-rnd lattice st: (Remove the slit marker as you work.)
Rnd 1. *Ctr-dbl-dec, yo, yo. Rep from * to end.
Rnd 2. *K2, p1. Rep from * to end.
Rnd 3. P to end of rnd.
Rnd 4. K until 1 st before marker, sl the last st onto the right needle without knitting it, remove marker, replace the slipped st on the left needle, and place marker back on left needle, once more moving the start of the rnd 1 st to the right.
Rep Rnds 1–4 until the work from

the top of the shoulder measures 79 (80) 81 (82) 83 (84)cm [31 (31.5) 32 (32.25) 32.75 (33)in] long or approx. 30cm [12in] shorter than your desired full length. End with a Rnd 4, but don't move the marker.

Side Slit in Skirt
Set up for working the slit in one side of the skirt:
Rnd 1. P3, tw k2tog, yo, yo, *ctr-dbl-dec, yo, yo. Rep from * until 4 sts remain, k2tog, p2.
Rnd 2. K3, *k2, p1. Rep from * until 3 sts remain, k3.
Rnd 3. Purl to end of rnd.
Rnd 4. Knit to end of rnd.
Rep Rnds 1–4 once.

Now, turn the work and work back and forth again, so the next row will be on the wrong/purl side:
Next row (ws). Make 1 left, k2, p2tog, yo, yo, *p-ctr-dbl-dec, yo, yo. Rep from * until 5 sts remain, tw p2tog, k3.
Next row (rs). Sl 1 p-wise, k2 *k2, p1. Rep from * until 4 sts remain, k4.
Next row (ws). Sl 1 p-wise, k to end of row.
Nest row (rs). Sl 1 p-wise, k to end of row.

Now work even in lattice st, starting on ws:
Row 1 (ws). Sl 1 p-wise, k2, p2tog, yo, yo, *ctr-dbl-dec, yo, yo. Rep from * until 5 sts remain, tw p2tog, k3.
Row 2. Sl 1 p-wise, k2 *k2, p1. Rep from * until 4 sts remain, k4.
Row 3 (ws) and **Row 4.** Sl 1 p-wise, k to end of row.

Rep Rows 1–4 until the gown measures 110 (110) 111 (112) 113 (113)cm [43.25 (43.25) 43.75 (44) 44.5 (44.5)in] from the top of the shoulder down.

K4 rows, starting each with Sl 1 p-wise.

Bind off in knit from the ws.

Neckline
With 3mm (US 2.5) [UK 11] needles and starting on the rs of the back left shoulder pick up and knit approx 78 (78) 78 (80) 80 (80) sts around the neckline.
Work 4 rows: Sl 1 p-wise, k to end of row.

Bind off in knit from the ws.

I-Cord Ties
Knit 4 i-cord ties: Pick up 3 sts at one corner of the neckline/back opening with 3mm (US 2.5) [UK 11] needles and knit i-cord: K3, *move the 3 sts back onto the left needle and k3.
Rep from * until the tie measures 34cm [13.25in] held taut.

Bind off.

Work 3 more ties the same way: Knit a 2nd tie on the opposite corner of the neckband and 2 more to meet halfway down the back opening.

Finishing
You're done! All parts are assembled.

Work any loose ends into the fabric on wrong side.

Lace Polo → 134

A slipover vest in lattice knitting, made adjustable with i-cord ties at the sides

Erika Slipover

Sizes
XS (S) M (L) XL (XXL)

Measurements
Circumference (with side cords tied as tight as possible):
86 (93) 100 (107) 114 (121)cm
[approx 34 (36.5) 39.5 (42) 45 (47.5)in]
Length: 43 (44) 45 (46) 47 (48)cm
[approx 17 (17.25) 17.75 (18) 18.5 (19)in]

Needles
Circular needle 3mm (US 2.5) [UK 11], 60cm [24in]
Circular needle 3.5mm (US 4) [UK 9 or 10], 80cm [32in]
Tapestry needle for finishing.

Knitting Gauge/Tension
17 sts x 27 rows in pattern on 3.5mm (US 4) [UK 9 or 10] needles = 10 × 10cm (4 × 4in)

Yarn
Gepardgarn's Cotton Wool 5
Colour 321 (beige):
or
Galaxy Glow Merino
Colour Together Again:
250 (300) 350 (400) 450 (500)g

Info
The vest is worked from the top down. The front is worked first, and the back is picked up from the front shoulders. The neckband and the ties are worked last.

The lattice-stitch pattern is unusual and tricky, but once you have it in hand, it flows. Master it while making your test swatch.

The square hole of lattice stitch is a multiple of 4 rows and 3 sts, including a first st and 2 final (total 3) selvage stitches.

A selvage- or edge-stitch is worked by slipping the first st purlwise with the yarn in front of the needle. In the next row, from the wrong side, the same st is knitted.

Start with 2 knit rows for garter st.
Row 1 (ws). K to end of row.
Row 2 (rs). K to end of row.
Row 3 (ws). Knit 1, purl 2 together, yarn over (yo), yarn over, *purl a centred double decrease (p ctr dbl dec): Slip 2 sts, one by one, as if to knit, insert left needle in next-to-last st on right needle from front and slip both it and last st together onto left needle. Purl 3 together (those 2 sts and the next st), yarn over, yarn over. Repeat from * until 2 sts remain, k2.
Row 4 (rs). K1, *k2, p1. Rep from * to end of row. The 2nd knit st is worked into the first yarn-over from the previous row. The purl st is worked into the second yarn over. This seems unlikely but works neatly and easily.

Right Front Shoulder
Cast on 17 (17) 20 (20) 23 (23) sts on 3.5mm (US 4) [UK 9 or 10] needle.

Work even in lattice st:
Row 1 (ws). K to end of row.
Row 2 (rs). Sl 1 p-wise, k to end of row.
Row 3. K1, p2tog, yo, yo, *p ctr dbl dec, yo, yo. Rep from* until 5 sts remain, tw p2tog, k3.
Row 4. Sl 1 p-wise, k2, *k2, p1. Rep from * until 2 sts remain, k2.

Work Rows 1–4 a total 6 (6) 6 (6) 7 (7) times.

Now inc to form the neck opening at left:
Work these 8 rows:
Row 1 (ws). K to end of row.
Row 2 (rs). Sl 1 p-wise, k to end of row.
Row 3 (ws). K1, p2tog, yo, yo, *p ctr dbl dec, yo, yo.
Rep from * until 5 sts remain.
tw p2tog, k3.
Row 4. (Inc) Sl 1 p-wise, k2, *k2, p1. Rep from * until 2 sts remain, k1, make 1 rt, k1.
Row 5. (Inc) K1, make 1 left, k rest of row.
Row 6. (Inc) Sl 1 p-wise, k until 1 st remains, make 1 rt, k1.
Row 7. K1, p2tog, yo, yo, *p ctr dbl dec, yo, yo. Rep from * until 3 sts remain, tw p2tog, k1.
Row 8. Sl 1 p-wise, k2 *k2, p1. Rep from * until 2 sts remain, k1, make 1 rt, k1.
Total 21 (21) 24 (24) 27 (27) sts.

Break yarn and put all sts on a holder.

Left Front Shoulder
Cast on 17 (17) 20 (20) 23 (23) sts on 3.5mm (US 4) [UK 9 or 10] needles.

Work even in lattice st:
Row 1 (ws). Sl 1 p-wise, then k to end of row.
Row 2 (rs). K to end of row.
Row 3. Sl 1 p-wise, k2, p2tog, yo, yo, *p ctr dbl dec, yo, yo. Rep from * until 3 sts remain, tw k2tog, k1.
Row 4. K1, *k2, p1. Rep from * until 4 sts remain, k4.

Work Rows 1–4 a total 6 (6) 6 (6) 7 (7) times.

Now increase and shape the neck opening to the right. Work these 8 rows:
Row 1 (ws). Sl 1 p-wise, then k to end of row.
Row 2. K to end of row.
Row 3. Sl 1 p-wise, k2, p2tog, yo, yo, *p ctr dbl dec, yo, yo.
Rep from * until 3 sts remain, tw p2tog, k1.
Row 4. (Inc) K1, make 1 left, *k2, p1.
Rep from * until 4 sts remain. k4.
Row 5. (Inc) Sl 1 p-wise, K until 1 st remains, make 1 rt, k1.
Row 6. (Inc) K1, make 1 left, k to end of row.
Row 7. Sl 1 p-wise, k2, p2tog, yo, yo; *p ctr dbl dec, yo, yo. Rep from * until 3 sts remain,tw p2tog, k1.
Row 8. (Inc) K1, make 1 left, *k2, p1. Rep from * until 4 sts remain, k4.
Total 21 (21) 24 (24) 27 (27) sts.

Now join the front shoulder sections:
Next row (ws). Sl 1 p-wise, k until 1 st remains, make 1 rt, k1, cast on 11 sts, put the right shoulder sts back on the needle matching rs and ws, k1, make 1 left, and k to end of row.
Total 55 (55) 61 (61) 67 (67) sts.

Next row (rs). Sl 1 p-wise, k to end of row.
Next row (ws). Sl 1 p-wise, k2, p2tog, yo, yo, *p ctr dbl dec, yo, yo. Rep from * until 5 sts remain, then tw p2tog, k3.
Next row. Sl 1 p-wise, k2, *k2, p1. Rep from * until 4 sts remain, k4.

Now work lattice st while increasing on both sides.

First work 4 rows with an inc only in Row 4:
Row 1 (ws) and Row 2 (rs). Sl 1 p-wise, k to end of row.
Row 3. Sl 1 p-wise, k2, p2tog, yo, yo, *p ctr dbl dec, yo, yo. Rep from * until 5 sts remain, tw p2tog, k3.
Row 4. (Inc) Sl 1 p-wise, k2, make 1 left, *k2, p1. Rep from * until 4 sts remain, k1, make 1 rt, k3.
Total 57 (57) 63 (63) 69 (69) sts.

Now increase:
Row 1 (ws). (Inc) Sl 1 p-wise, k2, make 1 left, k until3 sts remain in row, make 1 rt, k3.
Row 2 (rs). (Inc) Sl 1 p-wise, k2, make 1 left, k until 3 sts remain in row, make 1 rt, k3.
Row 3. Sl 1 p-wise, k2, p2tog, yo, yo, *p ctr dbl dec, yo, yo. Rep from * until 5 sts remain, tw p2tog, k3.
Row 4. Sl 1 p-wise, k2, make 1 left, *k2, p1 and rep from * until 4 sts remain, k1, make 1 rt, k3.

Work Rows 1–4 total 2 (3) 3 (4) 4 (5) times = 69 (75) 81 (87) 93 (99) sts.

Work 6 rows, increasing on Rows 1–2:
Row 1 (ws). (Inc) Sl 1 p-wise, k2, make 1 left, k until 3 sts remain in row, make 1 rt, k3.
Row 2 (rs). (Inc) Sl 1 p-wise, k2, make 1 left, k until 3 sts remain in row, make 1 rt, k3.
Row 3. Sl 1 p-wise, k2, p2tog, yo, yo, *p ctr dbl dec, yo, yo. Rep from * until 5 sts remain, tw p2tog, k3.
Row 4. Sl 1 p-wise, k2, *k2, p1. Rep from * until 4 sts remain, k4.
Row 5. Sl 1 p-wise, k to end of row.
Row 6. Sl 1 p-wise, k to end of row.
Total 73 (79) 85 (91) 97 (103) sts.

Now, work even in lattice st (the same as Rows 3–6 above):
Row 1. Sl 1 p-wise, k2, p2tog, yo, yo, *p ctr dbl dec, yo, yo. Rep from * until 5 sts remain, tw p2tog, k3.
Row 2. Sl 1 p-wise, k2, *k2, p1. Rep from * until 4 sts remain, k4.
Row 3. Sl 1 p-wise, k to end of row.
Row 4. Sl 1 p-wise, k to end of row.
Rep Rows 1–4 until front piece measures 43 (44) 45 (46) 47 (48) cm [17 (17.25) 17.75 (18) 18.5 (19)in].

Change to 3mm (US 2.5) [UK 11] needles and k 4 rows.

Bind off in knit on wrong side.

Left Back Shoulder
Working on the right side, pick up and k17 (17) 20 (20) 23 (23) sts from the top of the left front shoulder on 3.5mm (US 4) [UK 9 or 10] needles.

Work these 6 rows:
Row 1 (ws). K to end of row.
Row 2 (rs). Sl 1 p-wise, k to end of row.
Row 3. K to end of row.
Row 4. Sl 1 p-wise, k to end of row.
Row 5. K1, p2tog, yo, yo, *p ctr dbl dec, yo, yo. Rep from *, until 5 sts remain, tw p2tog, k3.
Row 6. Sl 1 p-wise, k2 *k2, p1. Rep from * until 2 sts remain, k2.

Break yarn and put sts on a holder.

Right Back Shoulder
From the right side (knit side), pick up and knit 17 (17) 20 (20) 23 (23) sts from the top edge of the right front shoulder on size 3.5mm (US 4) [UK 9 or 10] needles.

Work these 8 rows:
Row 1 (ws). Sl 1 p-wise, k to end of row.
Row 2 (rs). K to end of row.
Row 3. Rep Row 1.
Row 4. Rep Row 2.
Row 5. Sl 1 p-wise, k2, p2 tog, yo, yo, *p ctr dbl dec, yo, yo. Rep from * until 3 sts remain, tw p2tog, k1.
Row 6. K1, *k2, p1. Rep from * until 4 sts remain, k4.
Row 7. Sl 1 p-wise, k to end of row, then cast on 21 sts at the end of row, replace the left shoulder sts on the needle and k them.
Row 8. Sl 1 p-wise, k to end of row.
Total 55 (55) 61 (61) 67 (67) sts.

Work down in lattice pattern:
Row 1. Sl 1 p-wise, k2, p2 tog, yo, yo. *p ctr dbl dec, yo, yo. Rep from * until 5 sts remain, tw p2tog, k3.
Row 2. Sl 1 p-wise, k2, *k2, p1. Rep from * until 4 sts remain, k 4.
Row 3. Sl 1 p-wise, k to end of row.
Row 4. Sl 1 p-wise, k to end of row.
Work Rows 1–4 total 8 (8) 8 (8) 9 (9) times.
Work Rows 1–2 again.

Follow directions for increasing on the front and work the rest of the back using directions for the front panel. .

Neckline
Starting with the outside of the left back section, pick up and knit approx 98 (98) 98 (98) 98 (98) sts (a multiple of 2) along the neck opening on 3.5mm (US 4) [UK 9 or 10] needles. Place a marker and join in a rnd. P 1 rnd, k 1 rnd, p 1 rnd, k 1 rnd, turn work around (optionally make a turn st) and bind off in k on the wrong side.

I-Cord Ties
There are 8 i-cord ties.

Pick up and k3 sts into 1 st at the top corner of one underarm on 3.5mm (US 4) [UK 9 or 10] needles, moving back and forth from front to back loop.

*Staying on the rs, move the 3 sts back to the left needle and k them again. Rep from * until the cord is 34cm [13.5in] long, stretched taut. Bind off.

Make 3 more i-cord ties the same way, on each top underarm corner. Make 4 more placed halfway down the side panels.

Finishing
No assembly necessary.

With a tapestry needle, sew loose ends into the wrong side.

Mega Erika Jumper

Size
XS (S) M (L) XL (XXL) XXXL

Measurements
Chest: 107 (112) 117 (122) 127 (132) 137cm [42 (44) 46 (48) 50 (52) 54in]
Length: 52 (52) 53 (53) 55 (55) 57cm [20.5 (20.5) 21 (21) 21.75 (21.75) 22.5in]
Sleeve length, all sizes: 45cm [17.75in]

Needles
Circular needle 4.5mm (US 7) [UK 7], 60cm [24in]
Circular needle 6mm (US 10) [UK 4], 60cm [24in]
If not using the Magic Loop technique, use double-pointed needles in the same sizes for any small circumferences.
Tapestry needle for finishing .

Knitting Gauge/Tension
12 sts x 18 rows in lattice stitch on 6mm (US 10) [UK 4] needles with both yarns held together = 10 × 10cm (4 × 4in)

Lattice stitch is a multiple of 3, including 2 selvage sts.

Yarn
Rauma Garn's Vams
Pink version: Colour 66 (light rosa)
Light blue version (See p. 62)**:**
Colour 50 (light jeans blue)
500 (550) 600 (650) 700 (750) 750g

worked together with

Rauma Garn's Plum or Filcolana's Tilia
Pink version: Tilia Colour 321 (sakura)
Light blue version (See p. 62)**:**
Plum, Colour 67 (pale blue)
125 (150) 150 (175) 175 (200) 200g

Info
The sweater is worked from the top down.

The lattice-stitch pattern is unusual and tricky, but once you have it in hand, it flows. Master it while making your test swatch.

The square hole of lattice stitch is a multiple of 4 rows and 3 sts, including a first st and 2 final (total 3) selvage stitches.

The back is knitted first; then the front portion is picked up from the shoulders of the back portion. Finally, stitches are picked up for the sleeves and the neck.

Back Shoulders
Cast on 63 (66) 69 (72) 75 (78) 81 sts on 6mm (US 10) [UK 4] circular needle.
P1 row, but k the first and last sts.

Begin lattice pattern:
Row 1 (rs). K1, k2tog left, yo, yo, *ctr dbl dec, yo, yo. Rep from * until 3 sts remain, k2tog, k1.
Row 2 (ws). k1, p1, *k1, p2. Rep from * until 1 st remains, k1.
Row 3. K1, p until 1 st remains; k1.
Row 4. Rep Row 3.

Work Rows 1–4 a total 8 (8) 9 (9) 10 (10) 11 times.
Work Rows 1–2 again.
Break yarn and put sts on a holder.

Left Front Shoulder
Count 21 (21) 24 (24) 27 (27) 30 sts from the left side of the cast-on edge of the back in toward the centre of the back. The right side of the back should be toward you as you count.

Pick up and knit 21 (21) 24 (24) 27 (27) 30 sts from the sts you counted and out toward the edge. K6 rows.

Next row (ws). K1, p until 1 st remains, k1.

Start lattice pattern:
Row 1 (rs). K1, k2tog left, yo, yo; *ctr dbl dec, yo, yo. Rep from * until 3 sts remain, k2tog, k1.
Row 2 (ws) K1, p1, *k1, p2. Rep from * until 1 st remains, k1.
Row 3. K1, p until 1 st remains, k1.
Row 4. Rep row 3.
Work Rows 1–4 a total 4 times.

Now inc at the start of the right side (rs) rows to form the front neck opening toward the right:
Row 1 (rs). K1, k2tog left, yo, yo, *ctr dbl dec, yo, yo. Rep from * until 3 sts remain, k2tog, k1.

Row 2 (ws). K1, p1, *k1, p2. Rep from * until 1 st remains, k1.
Row 3. K1, make 1 left, p1, make 1 left, p across until 1 st remains, k1.
Row 4. K1, p until 1 st remains, k1.
Row 5. K1, make 1 left, k1, yo, yo, *ctr dbl dec, yo, yo. Rep from * until 3 sts remain, k2tog, k1.
Row 6. K1, p1 , *k1, p2. Rep from * until 2 sts remain, p1, k1.
Row 7. K1, make 1 left, p1, make 1 left, p until 1 st remains, k1.
Row 8. K1, p until 1 st remains, k1.
Row 9. K1, make 1 left, k2tog left, yo, yo *ctr dbl dec, yo, yo. Rep from * until 3 sts remain, k2tog, k1.

Sizes XS, M, XL and XXXL only
Row 10. k1, p1, *k1, p2. Rep from * until 2 sts remain, p1, k1.

Sizes S, L and XXL only
Row 10. K1, p1 *k1, p2. Rep from * until 2 sts remain, p1, make 1 rt, k1. Total 28 (29) 31 (32) 34 (35) 37 sts.

All Sizes
Break yarns and place sts on a holder.

Right Front Shoulder
On the rs, pick up and knit 21 (21) 24 (24) 27 (27) 30 sts from the back right shoulder. Start at the outside corner and work toward the middle. The right side (knit- or outside) of the back should be facing you. K6 rows.

Next row (ws). K1, p until 1 st remains, k1.

Now begin lattice stitch pattern:
Row 1 (rs). K1, k2tog left, yo, yo, *ctr dbl dec, yo, yo. Rep from * until 3 sts remain, k2tog, k1.
Row 2. K1, p1, *k1, p2. Rep from *, until 1 st remains, k1.
Row 3. K1, p across until 1 st remains, k1.
Row 4. Rep Row 3.
Work Rows 1–4 a total 4 times.
Work Row 1 again.

Now increase at the end of right side rows to shape the neck opening toward the left:
Row 1 (ws). K1, p1, *k1, p2. Rep from * until 1 st remains, k1.
Row 2 (rs). K1, p until 2 sts remain, make 1 rt, p1, make 1 rt, k1.
Row 3. K1, p until 1 st remains, k1.
Row 4. K1, k2tog left, yo, yo, *ctr dbl dec, yo, yo. Rep from * until 2 sts remain, k1. make 1 rt, k1.
Row 5. K1, p2, *k1, p2. Rep from * until 1 st remains, k1.
Row 6. K1, p until 2 sts remain, make 1 rt, p1, make 1 rt, k1.
Row 7. K1, p until 1 st remains, k1.
Row 8. K1, k2tog left, yo, yo, *ctr dbl dec, yo, yo. Rep from * until 3 sts remain, k2tog, make 1 rt, k1.

Sizes XS, M, XL, XXXL only
Row 9. K1, p2, *k1, p2. Rep from * until 1 st remains, k1.

Sizes S, L, XXL only
Row 9. K1, make 1 left, p2, *k1, p2. Rep from * until 1 st remains, k1. Total 28 (29) 31 (32) 34 (35) 37 sts.

All Sizes
Row 10 (joining the front pieces).
K1, p until 2 sts remain, tw p2tog, cast on 9 (10) 9 (10) 9 (10) 9 sts at the end of this row, put the left front shoulder sts back on the needle, p the first 2 sts tog, p until 1 st remains in row, k1.
Row 11. K1, p until 1 st remains, k1.
Total 63 (66) 69 (72) 75 (78) 81 sts.

A chunky sweater in lattice knitting

From this point work even in lattice st:
Row 1 (rs). K1, K2tog left, yo, yo, *ctr dbl dec, yo, yo. Rep from * until 3 sts remain, k2tog, k1.
Row 2. K1, p1, *k1, p2. Rep from * until 1 st remains, k1.
Row 3. K1, p until 1 st remains, k1.
Row 4. Rep Row 3.
Work Rows 1–4 a total 3 (3) 4 (4) 5 (5) 6 times.
Work Rows 1–2 once more.

Join back and front sections:
Next row. P2 together, p until 2 sts remain, tw p2tog, cast on 3 sts (underarm), place marker (side marker), place sts of back section back on needles, p the first 2 sts tog, p until there are 2 sts left on the back piece, tw p2tog, cast on 3 sts (underarm), place marker for start of rnd and join into a rnd. Total 128 (134) 140 (146) 152 (158) 164 sts.
K 1 rnd.

Body
Work around in lattice st:
Rnd 1. K2tog left, yo, yo, *ctr-dbl-dec, yo, yo. Rep from * until 5 sts remain before side marker, k2tog, p3, k2tog left, yo, yo. Rep from * until 5 sts remain before end of rnd, k2tog, p3.
Rnd 2. *K2, p1. Rep from * until 4 sts before side marker, k4, *k2, p1. Rep from * until 4 sts before end of rnd, k4.
Rnd 3. P to end of rnd.
Rnd 4. K to end of rnd.

Work Rnds 1–4 a total 13 (13) 14 (14) 15 (15) 16 times until the back measured down the centre is 44 (44) 46 (46) 48 (48) 50cm [17.25 (17.25) 18 (18) 19.75in].

Work Rnds 1–2 again, then k2 rnds.

Change to 4.5mm (US 7) [UK 7] needles and work 1 rnd twisted st ribbing while increasing: *tw k1(k through back of st), p1, tw k1, make 1 rt. Rep from * as many times as possible and work tw k ribbing the rest of rnd.

Remove the rnd marker as you work. If the last st is a k st, make 1 rt again to bring the total sts to a multiple of 2.

From this point, continue tw k1, p1 ribbing until ribbing is 8cm [3.25in] long.

Work 2 rnds double-knitting:
Rnd 1. *Tw k1, sl 1 p-wise with yarn in front, rep from * to end of rnd.
Rnd 2. *Sl 1 p-wise with yarn in back of work, p1. Rep from * to end of rnd.

End with Italian bind off.

Sleeves
Both sleeves follow these instructions: Start in the centre of the 3 sts cast on at the underarm.
From the rs, with 6mm (US 10) [UK 4] needles, pick up and k54 (54) 57 (57) 63 (63) 66 sts around the edge of the armhole. (Pick up 2 or 3 sts for every hole in the lattice pattern.) The final number of sts must a multiple of 3. Join sts for circular knitting and place a marker.
K 1 rnd.

Work circularly in lattice st pattern:
Rnd 1. *Ctr-dbl-dec, yo, yo. Rep from *to end of rnd.
Rnd 2. *K2, p1. Rep from * to end of rnd.
Rnd 3. P to end of rnd.
Rnd 4. K until 1 st before marker. Sl the last st over to the rt needle without knitting it, remove marker, move the slipped st to left needle, replace marker. You've

shifted the beg of rnd 1 st to the right.
Work Rnds 1–4 a total 2 (2) 3 (3) 3 (4) 4 times.

Continue with lattice pattern while decreasing:
** **Next rnd.** (1st dec)*Ctr-dbl-dec, yo, yo. Rep from * until 6 sts remain,
then ctr-dbl-dec, ctr-dbl-dec, and pass the 2nd st on the right needle over the first, yo, yo.

Work Rnds 2–4 as before.
Now, work Rnds 1–4 without decs on the 1st rnd a total 2 times.

Next rnd. (2nd dec) Ctr-dbl-dec, ctr-dbl-dec, move the 2 resulting sts onto left needle, pass the innermost st over the outermost and move the resulting st back onto the right needle, yo, yo, *ctr-dbl-dec, yo, yo. Rep from * to end of rnd.

Work Rnds 2–4 as before.
Now work Rnds 1–4 without decs on the 1st rnd a total 1 time.**

Rep from ** to ** once more.
Total 42 (42) 45 (45) 51 (51) 54 sts.
Work Rnds 1–2 again.

K2 rnds and on the 2nd rnd, for sizes M, L, XL and XXL only, k2tog at end of rnd.

Change to 4.5mm (US 7) [UK 7] needles and work 8cm [3.25in] twisted rib (tw k1, p1).
Work 2 rnds double-knit as for the bottom edge of the body.

End with Italian bind off.

Neck
On 4.5mm (US 7) [UK 7] needles, pick up and knit a total 88 (90) 90 (92) 92 (94) 94 sts around the neck opening, starting on the right side of the neck in back:

Pick up and k20 (20) 22 (22) 24 (24) 26 sts across the back of the neck, 30 (30) 30 (30) 30 (30) 30 sts along the left shoulder side, 8 (10) 8 (10) 8 (10) 8 sts across the centre of the front, and 30 (30) 30 (30) 30 (30) 30 sts on the right shoulder side. Join into a rnd and place a marker.

Work 20 rnds of twisted rib (k1 through back loop, p1).

Turn the neckband inward and, working on the ws with 6mm (US 4) [UK 10] needles, k the first picked-up st at the base of the ribbing tog with the first st on the left needle. *Pick up the next picked-up st and knit it tog with the next st on the left needle, then pass the first st over the 2nd. (The first st is now bound off.) Rep from * until all neckband sts are bound off.

Finishing
With a tapestry needle, work all loose ends into the wrong side.

Icelandic Hilda → 88

Decadent Sweater

Sizes
XS (S) M (L) XL (XXL)

Measurements
Chest: 112 (119) 124 (130) 135 (141)cm
[44 (47) 48.75 (51) 53 (55.5)in]
Length: 50 (51) 52 (53) 54 (56)cm
[19.75 (20) 20.5 (21) 21.25 (22)in]
Sleeve Length: 37 (39) 39 (39) 39 (39)cm
[14.5 (15.5) 15.5 (15.5) 15.5 (15.5)in]

Needles
Circular needle 5.5mm (US 9)
[UK 6], 80cm [32in]
Tapestry needle for finishing .

Knitting Gauge/Tension
14 sts x 21 rows on 5.5mm (US 9)
[UK 6] needles in stockinette with both
yarns held together = 10 × 10cm (4 × 4in)

Yarn
Rauma Garn's Vams
Colour 67 (royal blue):
400 (450) 450 (500) 550 (600)g

held together with

Rauma Garn's Plum
Colour 135 (dark blue):
100 (100) 100 (100) 125 (125)g

Info
The sweater is knitted from the top down.

The first and last st in every row is a knit st.

The whole sweater is worked with the 2 yarns held together.

Back
Cast on 3 sts.
P1 row.

Now inc on both ends on both k and p sides:
Row 1 (rs). K1, make 1 left, k to 1 st before end of row, make 1 rt, k1.
Row 2 (ws). K1, p make 1 rt, p until 1 st remains, p make 1 left, k1.

Rep Rows 1–2 19 (20) 21 (22) 23 (24) times = 79 (83) 87 (91) 95 (99) sts.

Work even in stockinette (k on right side, p on wrong side) until the centre back measures 22 (23) 24 (25) 26 (27)cm [8.75 (9) 9.5 (9.5) 10.25 (10.5)in].
Break yarn and place sts on a holder.

Left Front Shoulder
Pick up and k39 (41) 43 (45) 47 (49) sts from the right side along the slanted shoulder line at top of the back.

Now dec to shape the left edge of the shoulder:
Row 1 (ws). K1, p until 1 st remains, k1.
Row 2 (rs). K to end of row.
Row 3. K1, p until 1 st remains, k1.
Row 4. K until 6 sts remain, k2tog, k4.

Rep these 4 rows 8 (9) 9 (9) 10 (10) times = 31 (32) 34 (36) 37 (39) sts.

Work 3 (5) 7 (7) 9 (9) rows of stockinette.

Now inc to shape the right neck edge:
Row 1 (rs). (Inc) K4, make 1 left, k to end of row.
Row 2 (ws) K1, p until 1 st remains, k1.

Rep these 2 rows a total 4 (4) 4 (5) 5 (5) times = 35 (36) 38 (41) 42 (44) sts.

Break yarn and place sts on a holder.

Right Front Shoulder
From the rs of the slanted edge at the top of the back piece, pick up and k39 (41) 43 (45) 47 (49) sts.

Now dec to shape the left edge of the front:
Row 1 (ws). K1, p until 1 st remains, k1.
Row 2 (rs). K to end of row.
Row 3. K1, p until 1 st remains, k1.
Row 4. (Dec) K4, k2tog left, k to end of row.

Work Rows 1–4 a total 8 (9) 9 (10) 10 (10) times = 31 (32) 34 (36) 37 (39) sts.

Work 3 (5) 7 (7) 9 (9) rows in stockinette.

Now make incs to shape the left side of the neck opening, starting on the right side:
Row 1 (rs). K until 4 sts remain, make 1 rt, k4.
Row 2. K1, p until 1 st remains, k1.

Work Rows 1–2 total 4 (4) 4 (5) 5 (5) times. Total 35 (36) 38 (41) 42 (44) sts.

Join the front sections:
On the right shoulder, k to end of row, cast on 9 (11) 11 (9) 11 (11) sts, place the left shoulder sts on the needle, right sides matching, and knit them.
Total 79 (83) 87 (91) 95 (99) sts.

Work even in stockinette until the front measures 36 (37) 37 (38) 39 (40)cm [14 (14.5) 14.5 (15) 15.25 (15.75)in], measured from the point where sts were picked up at the shoulder.
End with a p row on the ws, starting and ending the row with k1.

Join the back and front sections:
K across the front section until 1 st remains, Add the back sts to the needle and k the last st of the front tog with the first st of the back.

K the back sts until 1 st remains and k the last back st tog with the first st of the front piece. Place a marker after this st as the start of the round.
Total 156 (164) 172 (180) 188 (196) sts.

Work the body circularly now in stockinette: You will always k and always from the right side.

Work even until the work from the top of the back measures 30 (31) 32 (33) 35 (36) cm [11.75 (12.25)12.5 (13) 13.75 (14)in].

The 'Shirt Tails'
Divide the work again into front and back: From the rnd marker, k76 (80) 84 (88) 92 (96) sts (the front); bind off 4 sts, k74 (78) 82 (86) 90 (94) sts and set these (the back) on a holder. Bind off 4 sts.
There are now 74 (78) 82 (86) 90 (94) each for the front and the back.
On the front, working back and forth again, work 4 rows in stockinette.

Now, dec on both sides:
Row 1. K4, k2tog left, k until 6 sts remain in row, k2tog, k4.
Row 2. K1, p until 1 st remains, k1.
Row 3. K to end of row.
Row 4. K1, p until 1 st remains, k1.
Work Rows 1–4 a total 5 (5) 5 (5) 6 (6) times.
Work Row 1 once more.
Break yarn and place sts on a holder.
62 (66) 70 (74) 76 (80) sts.

Replace the back section onto the needle and work the back sts the same way as the front.
Break yarn and place the sts on a holder.

Now set up to knit an i-cord edge:
Attach yarn at the top of the right slit to the left of the bound-off sts.

Pick up and k16 (16) 16 (16) 18 (18) sts from the right side along the vertical part of the slit, skipping every 3rd loop. K and mark the first st of the horizontal k sts of the front with a marker (the corner st), then k until 1 st remains of the front sts and mark the last st (another corner st).

Pick up and k16 (16) 16 (16) 18 (18) sts on the vertical edge of the left slit, pick up and k3 sts in the bound-off sts and k16 (16) 16 (16) 18 (18) sts down the other side of the left slit. Place the sts from the back portion back on the needles, k them, mark the first and last sts as on the front, and pick up and k16 (16) 16 (16) 18 (18) sts along the vertical edge of the slit and finally, pick up and k3 sts along the bound-off sts at the top of the slit.

Break yarn and re-attach it. (It's important to break the yarn here, for the finished product to look the very best.)

Working an i-cord edging:
Start by knitting 4 sts into the first st in the slit, where you started picking up sts. Do this by knitting into the back, then the front of the first st, back and forth, twice. Stay on the right side and replace these 4 sts back on the left needle, one by one.

Next row. *K3, tw k2tog (1 cast-on st with 1 picked-up st), set 4 sts back on left needle, one by one. (In this way you're continually adding 1 st from the knitted edge into the i-cord and binding it off at the same time.) Rep from * until you reach the first corner st. Now work the corner: K4 sts and (without digging into sts of the knit edge), replace the 4 sts back on the left needle, one by one, then k3, tw k2tog (now include a st from the knit edge), replace the 4 sts on the left needle, one by one, k4, replace the 4 sts on the left needle, one by one.

Now work the i-cord as first described up to the next corner stitch and knit around this corner just as you did the first one. Rep along the entire edge until the whole bottom edge is bound off with i-cord.

Finally, bind off the 4 i-cord sts one by one.

Sleeves
Starting at the centre cast-on underarm st, pick up and k approx 56 (58) 58 (60) 62 (64) sts around the armhole on 5.5mm (US 9) [UK 6] needle. (Skip every 4th loop on the vertical sides of the armhole.) Join into a rnd and place a marker for beg of rnd.

A lighter, cropped oversize jumper with graphically shaped sleeves. The sweater has a V-neck in back and rounded 'shirt tails' at the bottom.

Now dec to shape the outer side of the sleeve:
Rnds 1–15. Knit.
Rnd 16. (Dec) K1, k2tog rt, k until 3 sts before marker, tw k2tog left, k1.

Work Rnds 1–16 a total 3 times.
Total 50 (52) 52 (54) 56 (58) sts.
K1 more rnd and place a marker after the first 25 (26) 26 (27) 28 (29) sts.

Now dec around the new marker:
Rnd 1–3. K to end of rnd.
Rnd 4. K to 3 sts before the marker, tw k2tog left, k2, k2tog, k to end of rnd.

Work Rnds 1–4 a total 6 (7) 7 (7) 7 (7) times = 38 (38) 38 (40) 42 (44) sts.

Continue even until sleeve is 37 (39) 39 (39) 39 (39)cm [14.5 (15.5) 15.5 (15.5) 15.5 (15.5)in] long, or your desired length.

Now work an i-cord edging:
Start by knitting 4 sts in the first st of the rnd by knitting alternately into the front and back loops of 1 st.

*Place the 4 sts back on the left needle one by one (staying on the k side), k3, tw k2tog (including the next st of the sleeve itself), k3, tw k2tog. Rep from * until all sleeve sts are bound off into the i-cord. Bind off the i-cord sts one by one.

Break yarn with a 10cm [4in] tail.

K the other sleeve following the same directions.

Neckline I-Cord Edging
Starting at the top of the left front shoulder, pick up and k94 (96) 98 (100) 102 (104) sts around the neck opening from the rs on 5.5mm (US 9) [UK 6] needle. Skip about every 4th st on the vertical sides but pick up every cast-on st in the front of the neck opening. Break yarn.

Now, knit an i-cord edging around the neck opening, which will start narrow and grow wider.

Join the yarn again in the left shoulder piece.

IMPORTANT: After every 'rnd,' all the i-cord sts are slipped, one by one, back onto the left needle, so all rows start on the rs, as on the bottom edge and the sleeves' i-cord edgings.

Rnd 1. K2 sts in the first st of the neck edge (1 in front loop, one in back loop).
Rnd 2. K1, tw k2tog.
Rnd 3. K1, tw k2tog.
Rnd 4. (Inc) K1, make 1 rt, tw k2tog.
Total 3 sts
Rnd 5. K2, tw k2tog.
Rnd 6. K2, tw k2tog.
Rnd 7. (Inc) K1, make 1 rt, k1, tw k2tog. Total 4 sts
Rnd 8. *K3, tw k2tog.
Sl sts back to left needle, one by one.*

Rep from * to * until there are 6 neck edge sts left on the needle, beside the 4 i-cord sts.

Now dec to narrow the i-cord again.
Remember to move the i-cord sts back onto the left needle, one by one after every row.
Row 1. K2tog, k1, tw k2tog.
Row 2. K2, tw k2tog.
Row 3. K2, tw k2tog.
Row 4. K2tog, tw k2tog.
Row 5. K1, tw k2tog.
Row 6. K1, tw k2tog.
Bind off.

Finishing
With tapestry needle, work all loose ends into the ws surface and sew ends of i-cords into their fabric with duplicate stitch.

Wash and block according to yarn manufacturer's instructions.

Take care to block the bottom all the way to the edge, to keep the i-cord edge from curling.

Decadent Dress

Sizes
XS (S) M (L) XL (XXL)

Measurements
Chest: 112 (119) 124 (130) 135 (141)cm
[44 (47) 49 (51) 53 (55.5)in]
Length: 103 (105) 107 (109) 110 (111)cm
[40.5 (41.25) 42 (43) 43.25 (43.75)in]
Sleeve Length: 37 (39) 39 (39) 39 (39)cm
[14.5 (15.25) 15.25 (15.25) 15.25 (15.25)in]

Needles
Circular needle 5.5mm (US 9) [UK 5], 80cm [32in]. If not using Magic Loop technique, use double-pointed needles in the same size for the sleeves.
Tapestry needle for finishing.

Knitting Gauge/Tension
14 sts x 21 rows on 5.5mm (US 9) [UK 6] needles in stockinette with both yarns held together = 10 × 10cm (4 × 4in)

Yarns
Rauma Garn's Vams
Colour 03 (light gray heather):
700 (750) 750 (800) 850 (900)g

held together with

Rauma Garn's Plum
Colour 055 (light beige):
150 (150) 150 (175) 175 (200)g

Info
The dress is worked from the top down. The first and last st of every row is a knit st. The whole garment is worked with the 2 yarns held together.

Work the Decadent Dress following directions for Decadent Sweater on p. 37 to the point where the pattern says, 'Knit the body circularly in stockinette.'

From there, work straight down until your work measures 82 (84) 86 (88) 88 (89)cm [32.25 (33) 34 (34.75) 34.75 (35)in] from the top of the back, then continue as follows:

Side Slits
Divide the stitches into front and back sections:
K76 (80) 84 (88) 92 (96) sts (front), bind off 4 sts (side slit).
K74 (78) 82 (86) 90 (94) sts and place these sts (the back) on a holder, bind off 4 sts (side slit).
Total 74 (78) 82 (86) 90 (94) sts each for front and back.

Skirt
Work back and forth with 6 rows stockinette on the front, where first and last st of every row is a k st.

Now dec on both sides:
Row 1. K4, k2tog left, k until 6 sts remain, k2tog, k to end of row.
Rows 2–6. Work stockinette back and forth, knitting on rs, purling on ws with a k st at beg and end each row.

Work Rows 1–6 a total 5 (5) 5 (5) 6 (6) times.
Work working Row 1 once more.
Total 62 (66) 70 (74) 76 (80) sts.

Break yarn and place sts on a holder. Replace the back sts on needles and work the back exactly like the front. Break yarn at the end and place sts on a holder.

Set up for an i-cord edging:
Attach yarn again at the top of the right slit, left of the bound-off sts.

Pick up and k20 (20) 20 (20) 22 (22) sts along the vertical edge of the right slit. (Skip every 3rd st vertically.)

Place a marker at the first st of the live front edge (a corner st).

K until 1 st remains on the front bottom edge; k and place a marker on the last live front stitch (corner stitch).

Pick up and k20 (20) 20 (20) 22 (22) sts along the vertical edge of the left slit, pick up and k the 3 bound-off sts at top of slit.

Pick up and k20 (20) 20 (20) 22 (22) sts down the other side of the slit.

Replace the sts of the back on the needle, k and place a marker on the first and last sts of the back bottom edge (corner sts) as you did on the front edge, then pick up and k20 (20) 20 (20) 22 (22) sts up along the back vertical edge of the slit and finally, pick up and k3 sts along the bound-off sts at the top. Break yarn.

I-Cord Edging
Attach the yarn at the first st you picked up in the slit and start by knitting 4 sts into this stitch, alternating between the front and the back loop. Staying on the knit side, replace the 4 sts back on the left needle one by one.
Next row. *K3, tw k2tog (including 1 st from the picked up sts), slip the 4 sts back on the left needle, one by one. (In this way, 1 st from the knitted edge is constantly added to the i-cord and bound off.)
Rep from * until you reach the first corner st.

Now work the corner:
K4 sts and (without digging into sts of the knit edge), replace the 4 sts back on the left needle, one by one, then k3, tw k2tog (now including a st from the knit edge), replace the 4 sts on the left needle, one by one, k4, replace the 4 sts on the left needle, one by one. (2 i-cord sts unattached to work, between them 1 st attached to corner.)

Now work the i-cord as described, up to the next corner stitch and knit around this corner just as you did the first one. Rep along the entire edge until the whole bottom edge is bound off with i-cord.

Finally, bind off the 4 i-cord sts one by one. Break yarn.

Sleeves
Starting at the bottom of the armhole, pick up and k about 56 (58) 58 (50) 62 (64) sts around the armhole on 5.5mm(US 9) pUK 5] needles, skipping every 4th st on the vertical parts. Join as a rnd and place a rnd marker.

Dec to shape the inner side of the sleeve as follows:
Rnds 1–15. Knit.
Rnd 16. (Dec) K1, k2tog, k until 3 sts before marker, k2tog left, k1.
Work Rnds 1–16 a total 3 times = 50 (52) 52 (54) 56 (58) sts.

K1 more rnd and place a marker after the first 25 (26) 26 (27) 28 (29) sts.

Now dec around the new marker:
Rnds 1–3. Knit to end of rnd.
Rnd 4. K until 3 sts before marker, k2tog left, k2, k2tog, k to end of rnd.

Work Rows 1 to 4 total 6 (7) 7 (7) 7 (7) times.
Total 38 (38) 38 (40) 42 (44) sts.
Don't break yarn.

Now work an i-cord edging as follows:
Start by knitting 4 sts into the first st by knitting alternately into its front and back loops. *Put these 4 sts back on the left needle, one by one (staying on the knit side), k3, tw k2tog (including a st from the knitted edge).* Rep * to * until all edge sts are bound off with i-cord. Bind off the 4 i-cord sts one by one at the end.

K the other sleeve following the same directions.

Neckline
Follow directions on p. 39 for finishing Decadent Sweater's neck line with i-cord edging.

Finishing
Sew all loose ends into the purl side and sew the i-cord tails in with duplicate st.

Wash and block the dress following yarn manufacturer's instructions. Take care to block out to the edges of the hemline to keep the i-cord edges from rolling.

A light, oversize dress with graphically shaped sleeves, a v-neck and slits on both sides

Lykke Jumper

Sizes
XS (S) M (L) XL (XXL)

Measurements
Chest: 112 (117) 120 (125) 132 (135)cm
[44 (46) 47.25 (49.25) 52 (53.125)in]
Length: 44 (45) 51 (52) 52 (56)cm
[17.25 (17.75) 20 (20.5) 22 in]

Needles
Circular needle 4.5mm (US 7)
[UK 7], 60cm [24in]
Circular needle 6mm (US 10)
[UK 4], 60cm [24in]
If not using Magic Loop technique, use double-pointed needles in the same sizes.
Tapestry needle for finishing.

Knitting Gauge/Tension
12 sts x 20 rows on 6mm (US 10)
[UK 4] needles in stockinette with both yarns held together = 10 × 10cm (4 × 4in)

Yarns
Sandnes' KOS
Colour 2390 (forest brown):
300 (300) 300 (350) 350 (350)g

held together with

Sandnes' Tynn Silk Mohair
Colour 3880 (dark chocolate):
100 (100) 125 (150) 150 (150)g

Info
Knitted from the top down. The sweater is knitted with both yarns held together throughout.

The whole project with the exception of the ribbed edges, is worked in the following 12 rnd pattern, which repeats:

Rnds 1–6. K to end of rnd.
Rnd 7. *Yarn over (yo), k1. Rep from * to end of rnd.
Rnd 8. K to end of rnd, dropping all yarn overs.
Rnd 9. Rep Rnd 7.
Rnd 10. Rep Rnd 8.
Rnd 11. Rep Rnd 7.
Rnd 12. Rep Rnd 8.

Neck
Cast on 68 (70) 72 (74) 74 (76) sts loosely on 4.5mm (US 7) [UK 7] needles. Join for circular knitting and place marker.

Work 11 rnds in k1, p1 ribbing.
P1 rnd.
Work 10 rnds in k1, p1 ribbing.

Work 1 more rnd in k1, p1 ribbing and place markers after 9 (9) 10 (10) 10 (11) sts (left sleeve); after 25 (26) 26 (27) 27 (27) sts (front portion); 9 (9) 10 (10) 10 (11) sts (right sleeve); 25 (26) 26 (27) 27 (27) sts (back).

Start raglan increases:
Change to 6mm (US 10) [UK 4] needles, and start pattern rnds, while making raglan incs. *NOTE:* The sts next to the markers are knit without yo's in any rnd.

Rnd 1. *K1, make 1 left, k to 1 st before marker, make 1 rt. Rep from * 3 more times.
Rnd 2. K to end of rnd.

Work Rnds 1–2 a total 19 (20) 21 (22) 23 (24) times = 220 (230) 240 (250) 258 (268) sts.

Work 0 (0) 7 (7) 7 (4) rnds in pattern without incs.
Total 47 (49) 52 (54) 56 (59) 61 sts for each sleeve and 63 (66) 68 (71) 73 (75) sts each for front and back portions.

Body
Divide work into front, back and sleeves: Place left sleeve sts on a holder, cast on 4 (4) 4 (4) 6 (6) sts for left underarm (Set a marker in the centre of these to mark the beg of rnds.), k across front, place right sleeve sts on a holder, cast on 4 (4) 4 (4) 6 (6) sts for right underarm, knit back sts. Total 134 (140) 144 (150) 158 (162) sts for body.

Work even in pattern until you've worked the 12 pattern rnds a total 5 (5) 6 (6) 6 (7) times from top to bottom of the sweater.
K6 rnds.

Change to 4.5mm (US 7) [UK 7] needles and work 8 (11) 11 (14) 14 (14) rnds in k1, p1 ribbing. Bind off loosely in k1, p1 ribbing.

Sleeves
Place the sts for one sleeve back on the larger size needle:
Starting at the centre of the underarm, pick up and k2 (2) 2 (2) 3 (3) sts from left group of cast-on underarm sts, work the sleeve sts, then pick up and k the remaining 2 (2) 2 (2) 3 (3) cast-on sts of the underarm, place marker, and join in a rnd.
Total 51 (53) 56 (58) 62 (65) sts.

Work even, until the 12 pattern rnds are worked a total 7 (7) 8 (8) 8 (9) times, or to desired length.
K6 rnds.

Change to 4.5mm (US 7) [UK 7] needles and k2tog completely around. If you end on an uneven number of sts, k2tog once more. Work 8 (11) 11 (14) 14 (14) rnds k1, p1 ribbing. Bind off in ribbing.

Knit the opposite sleeve to match.

Assembly
Fold neckband over to the inside and sew it down. Work all ends into the inside.

An oversize sweater with a boxy fit with generous sleeves and a big rollover collar

Bibi Sweater

Sizes
XS (S) M (L) XL (XXL)

Measurements
Bust: 103 (115) 126 (132) 144 (150)cm
[40.5 (45.25) 49.5 (52) 56.75 (59)in]
Sweater length: 54 (55) 57 (58) 59 (60)cm
[21.5 (21.75) 22.5 (23)23.25 (23.75)in]
Sleeve length: 44 (44) 44 (45) 45 (45)cm
[17.25 (17.25) 17.25 (17.75) 17.75 (17.75)in]

Needles
Circular needle 2.5mm (US 1.5)
[UK 12 or 13], 60cm [24in]
Circular needle 3.5mm (US 4)
[UK 9 or 10], 100cm [40in]
If not using Magic Loop technique, use double-pointed needles in each size for sleeves.
Tapestry needle for finishing.

Knitting Gauge/Tension
26 sts x 29 rnds on 3.5mm (US 4)
[UK 9 or 10] needles with both yarns held together = 10 × 10cm (4 × 4in)

Yarns
Filcolana's Saga
held together with
Filcolana's Tilia
(See specific colours to right)

For a wider colour selection, you might swap Ficolana's Arwetta Classic for Saga. In the pink sweater shown here, we used Arwetta for Colour F.

Info
The sweater is worked from the bottom up.

Colour pattern knitting is also called Fair Isle. If you usually carry the yarn in your left hand, work with both colours over your left index finger always in the same order. The colour closest to you (and the needle) will dominate visually, the other, usually the lighter colour, will recede somewhat. There is no twisting involved and the yarn not in use will run straight across the purl side. Be careful not to pull either yarn tight when changing colours. If you carry the yarns in your right hand, always bring the dominant colour from beneath the other and the secondary colour *over* the dominant. If you are comfortable with both styles of knitting, you can pick the dominant (darker) color from your left index and carry the secondary color on your right index to accomplish the same effect.

Yarns (Blue Sweater)
Each colour has 2 strands held (and knitted) as one.
Colour A
Saga, Colour 212: 100 (100) 150 (150) 200 (200)g;
Tilia, Colour 145: 75 (75) 100 (100) 125 (125)g.
Colour B
Saga, Colour 302: 100 (100) 150 (150) 200 (200)g;
Tilia, Colour 321: 75 (75) 100 (100) 125 (125)g.
Colour C
Saga, Colour 977: 50 (50) 100 (100) 100 (100)g;
Tilia, Colour 101: 25 (25) 75 (75) 75 (75)g.
Colour D
Saga, Colour 301: 50 (50) 50 (50) 50 (50)g;
Tilia, Colour 340: 25 (25) 25 (25) 25 (25)g.
Colour E
Saga, Colour 110: 50 (50) 50 (50) 50 (50)g;
Tilia, Colour 325: 25 (25) 25 (25) 25 (25)g
Colour F
Saga, Colour 117: 50 (50) 50 (50) 50 (50)g;
Tilia, Colour 322: 25 (25) 25 (25) 25 (25)g
Colour G
Arwetta Classic, Colour 251: 50 (50) 50 (50) 50 (50)g;
Tilia, Colour 196: 25 (25) 25 (25) 25 (25)g

Yarns (Pink Sweater)
Each colour has 2 strands held (and knitted) as one.
Colour A
Saga, Colour 302: 100 (100) 150 (150) 200 (200)g;
Tilia, Colour 321: 75 (75) 100 (100) 125 (125)g.
Colour B
Saga, Colour 353: 100 (100) 150 (150) 200 (200)g;
Tilia, Colour 353: 75 (75) 100 (100) 125 (125)g.
Colour C
Saga, Colour 977: 50 (50) 50 (50) 50 (50)g;
Tilia, Colour 101: 25 (25) 25 (25) 25 (25)g.

Colour D
Saga, Colour 301: 50 (50) 50 (50) 50 (50)g;
Tilia, Colour 340: 25 (25) 25 (25) 25 (25)g.
Colour E
Saga, Colour 110: 50 (50) 100 (100) 100 (100)g;
Tilia, Colour 325: 25 (25) 50 (50) 50 (50)g.
Colour F
Arwetta Colour 251: 50 (50) 50 (50) 50 (50)g;
Tilia, Colour 196: 25 (25) 25 (25) 25 (25)g.
Colour G
Saga, Colour 277: 50 (50) 50 (50) 50 (50)g;
Tilia, Colour 218: 25 (25) 25 (25) 25 (25)g.
Colour H
Saga, Colour 376: 100 (100) 150 (150) 200 (200)g;
Tilia, Colour 279: 75 (75) 100 (100) 125 (125)g.

Body
Using Italian cast-on, cast on 268 (300) 328 (344) 372 (388) sts on 2.5mm (US 1.5) [UK 12 or 13] needle with Colour A. Place marker and join into a rnd.

Work 2 rnds double-knit:
Rnd 1. *Tw k1, sl 1 p-wise with yarn in front. Rep from * to end of rnd.
Rnd 2. *Sl 1 p-wise with yarn behind work, p1. Rep from * to end of rnd.

Change to k2, p2 ribbing.
Rib even around and continue ribbing until ribbing measures 6 (6) 6 (6) 7 (7) cm [2.5 (2.5) 2.5 (2.5) 2.75 (2.75)in].

Change to 3.5mm (US 4) [UK 9 or 10] needle and k 1 rnd, increasing 2 (0) 2 (1) 3 (2) sts evenly distributed around.
Total 270 (300) 330 (345) 375 (390) sts.

Start pattern chart and repeat it across each rnd. Work even in pattern and stockinette until the work, including the ribbing, measures 31 (32) 33 (34) 35 (36)cm [12.25 (12.5) 13 (13.5) 13.75 (14.25)in].

Now bind off for the underarm opening:
K133 (148) 163 (170) 185 (193) sts (front), bind off 2 sts for rt underarm, k133 (148) 163 (171) 186 (193) sts (back), bind off 2 (2) 2 (2) 2 (2) sts for left underarm.
Next rnd. Cast on 3 sts with both colours (4 strands, 2 of each colour) to start a steek and to continue working circularly. K in pattern across the front portion, cast on 3 sts in the same way at 2nd underarm and work colour pattern across the back.
Total 272 (302) 332 (347) 377 (392) sts.

The 3 sts cast on on at each side are now purled with both colours together in all rnds. Work up in pattern until the whole project measures 47 (48) 50 (51) 53 (54)cm [18.5 (19) 19.75 (20) 20.75 (21.25)in].

Neckline
Next rnd. P the 3 steek sts, k 50 (57) 64 (67) 74 (76) sts, bind off 33 (34) 35 (36) 37 (41) sts and continue to end of rnd as before.

Break yarn and re-attach it from the knit side onto the right side of the sts bound off for the neck opening. Now work back and forth, still in pattern.

Next row (rs). Bind off 3 sts, k to end of row.
Next row (ws). Bind off 3 sts, p to end of row.
Next row (rs). Bind off 2 sts, k to end of row.
Next row (ws). Bind off 2 sts, p to end of row.
***Next row (rs).** Bind off 1 st, k to end of row.
Next row (ws). Bind off 1 st, p to end of row.*

Work rows * to * a total 3 times.
Total 223 (252) 281 (295) 324 (335) sts divided into: 42 (49) 56 (59) 66 (68) sts each front shoulder, 6 steek sts (3 on each side) and 133 (148) 163 (171) 186 (193) sts for the back.

Knit even until body measures 54 (55) 57 (58) 60 (61)cm [21.25 (21.75) 22.5 (22.75) 23.625 (24)in].

Next row. K 1 row and bind off the steek sts and the centermost 49 (50) 51 (53) 54 (57) sts of the back. Place remaining sts to rest on a holder.

Finishing the Body
With tapestry needle, work all loose ends into wrong side of fabric. With a sewing machine, sew over steek sts lengthwisse, so there are stitches in every p st lying closest to the armhole. You can sew across the p sts twice.

Cut lengthwise through the middle of the centre st between sewing machine stitches to open the armholes.

Knitting the shoulder seams together:
Turn the body inside out. Place the front right shoulder sts on a separate needle so

that the right front portion and the right back shoulder are each on their own needle. (These can be 2 ends of the circular needle.)

Hold the needles together in the left hand with the right sides facing.

With a third needle (the same size as you've been using if you have one. If not, the needle used for ribbing will work.), k the first sts together, one from each needle.

K the next 2 sts tog, one from each needle, then bind off by passing the first st over the second. Continue this until you have knit tog and bound off all the sts. Repeat on the left shoulder.

Sleeves
The chart for the sleeves starts where the body chart left off when the 2 sts on each side were bound off at the underarm. Work the chart from the top down instead of from the bottom up.

Pick up and k 120 (120) 120 (135) 135 (135) sts around the armhole with the colour that works best with that point in the chart, join for circular knittinng and place a marker at centerpoint of the underarm for the beg of the rnd.

Work even down the sleeve in stockinette and in pattern until the sleeve is 38 (38) 38 (39) 39 (39)cm [15 (15) 15 (15.5) in] long while decreasing every 10th (10th) 10th (7th) 7th (7th) rnd, a total 12 (12) 12 (16) 16 (16) times by:
k2tog, k until 2 sts remain in rnd, k2tog left. K dec sts in the colour that fits into the colour pattern.
Total 96 (96) 96 (103) 103 (103) sts.

Change to 2.5mm (US 1.5) [UK 12 or 13] needles and k 1 rnd with Colour A, and inc 0 (0) 0 (1) 1 (1) st at the beg of row by make 1 rt.

Work 6cm [2.5in] k2, p2 ribbing, then 2 rnds double-knit (see above under Body).

Bind off with Italian bind-off.

Rollover Collar
Pick up and k120 sts on 2.5mm (US 1.5) [UK 12 or 13] needles with Colour A. Pick up about 1 st in every neckline st. Work 24cm [9.5in] in k2, p2 ribbing.

Work 2 rnds double-knit and bind off with Italian bind-off.

Finishing
Work yarn ends into ws of sleeves.

Wash sweater according to yarn manufacturer's instructions and block sweater as it dries.

Chart for Bibi in blue

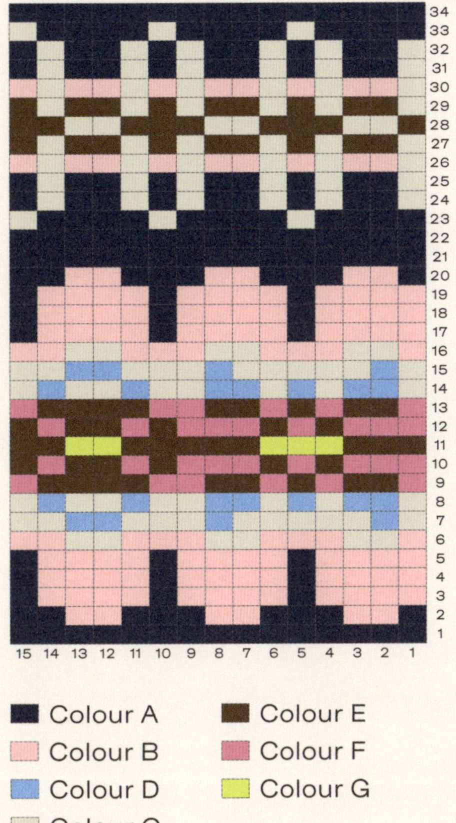

Chart for Bibi in pink

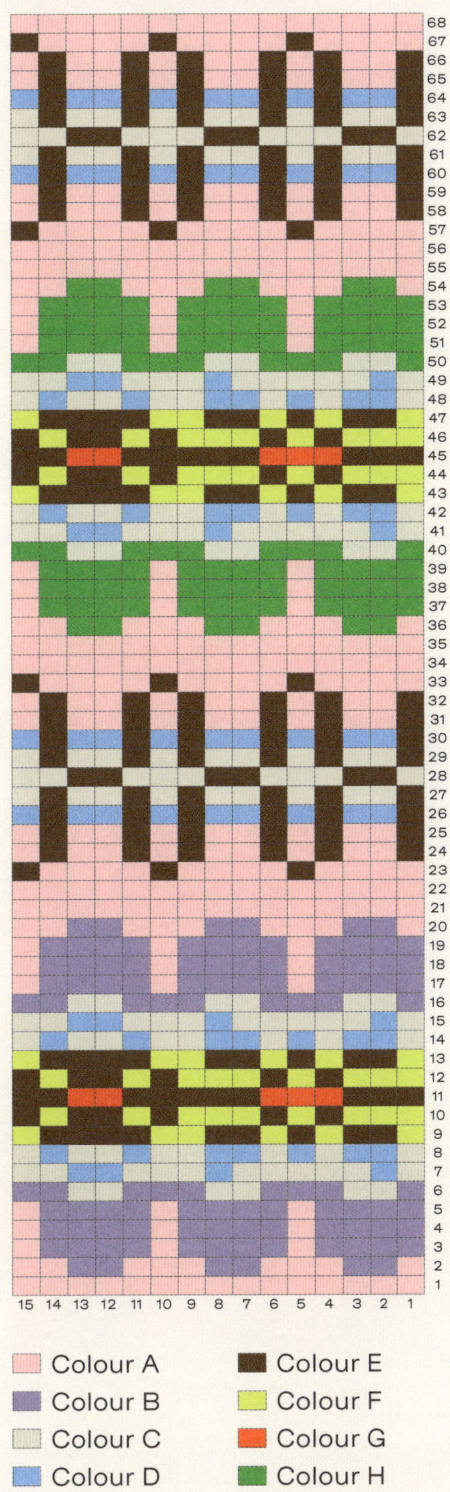

Mega Bibi Slipover

Sizes
XS-S (M-L) XL-XXL

Measurements
Chest: 100 (117) 133cm
[39.25 (46) 52.5in]
Length: 51 (54) 56cm
[20 (21.25) 22in]

Needles
Circular needle 3.5mm (US 4) [UK 9 or 10], 60cm [24in]
Circular needle 5.5mm (US 9) [UK 5], 80cm [32in]

Knitting Gauge/Tension
18 sts x 19 rnds on 5.5mm (US 9) [UK 5] needles in pattern with 2 strands of each color held together = 10 × 10 cm (4 × 4in) You are then knitting with 4 strands of each pair of colours.

Yarn
2 strands of Ficolana's Saga yarn are held with 2 strands of Ficolana's Tilia yarn throughout. You can substitute Ficolana's Arwetta Classic for the Saga if you want a wider colour palette. In the slipover here, Arwetta was used for Colour G.

Colour A
Saga, Colour 212: 100 (100) 150g
Tilia, Colour 145: 50 (50) 75g
Colour B
Saga, Colour 302: 100 (100) 150g
Tilia, Colour 321: 50 (50) 75g
Colour C
Saga, Colour 977: 50 (50) 100g
Tilia, Colour 101: 50 (50) 75g
Colour D
Saga, Colour 301: 50 (50) 50g
Tilia, Colour 340: 25 (25) 25g
Colour E
Saga, Colour 110: 50 (50) 100g
Tilia, Colour 325: 50 (50) 75g
Colour F
Saga, Colour 117: 50 (50) 100g
Tilia, Colour 322: 25 (25) 50g
Colour G
Arwetta, Colour 251: 50 (50) 50g
Tilia, Colour 196: 25 (25) 25g

Info
The slipover is worked from the bottom up. The shoulders are sewn together before working ribbing on neckband and armholes.

Colour pattern knitting is also called Fair Isle. If you usually carry the yarn in your left hand, work with both colours over your left index finger always in the same order. The colour closest to you (and the needle) will dominate visually, the other, usually the lighter colour, will recede somewhat. There is no twisting involved and the yarn not in use will run straight across the purl side. Be careful not to pull either yarn tight when changing colours. If you carry the yarns in your right hand, always bring the dominant colour from beneath the other and the secondary colour *over* the dominant. If you are comfortable with both styles of knitting, you can pick the dominant (darker) color from your left index and carry the secondary color on your right index to accomplish the same effect.

Use the Bibi chart on p. 53.

Body
Using Italian cast-on, cast on 180 (208) 240 sts on 3.5mm (US 4) [UK 9 or 10] needle with Colour A. Join in a rnd and place a marker for beg of rnd.
Now work 2 rnds of double-knit:
Rnd 1. *K1, sl 1 p-wise with yarn in front of needle. Rep from * to end of rnd.
Rnd 2. *Sl 1 p-wise with yarn behind needle, p1. Rep from * to end of rnd.

Change to k2, p2 ribbing. Continue ribbing until ribbing measures 6cm [2.5in].

Change to 5.5mm (US 9) [UK 5] needle. K 1 rnd, increasing 0 (2) 0 sts evenly across rnd. Total 180 (210) 240 sts.

Start pattern chart at lower right and rep it to end of rnd.

Continue even in chart pattern and stockinette until your work, including ribbing, measures 22 (24) 26cm [8.75 (9.5) 10.25in].

A loose-fitting slipover vest in a blown-up Bibi pattern

Armhole
Next rnd. K84 (99) 114 sts (front), bind off 11 sts with both colours, k79 (94) 109 sts (back), put sts on a holder and bind off the next 11 sts. Total 79 (94) 109 sts each for front and back sections.

Now k back and forth in pattern and stockinette.

Continue the charted pattern to vertically fit the pattern established before the armhole bind-offs.

Front
Row 1 (rs). K to end of row.
Row 2 (ws). K1, p until 1 st remains, k1.

Now make decs to shape armholes:
Row 1 (rs): Bind off 1st st, k to end of row.
Row 2 (ws): Bind off 1st st, p until 1 st remains, k1.

Work Rows 1–2 a total 10 (14) 17 times. Total 59 (66) 75 sts.

From this point, work even in pattern and stockinette until work measures 41 (43) 45cm [16 (17) 17.75in] from cast-on edge.

Now divide work into right and left front pieces while binding off for neck opening: K22 (24) 27 sts and place these sts on a holder (right shoulder), bind off 15 (18) 21 sts (front neckline), k22 (24) 27 sts (left shoulder).

Work the left shoulder now:
Row 1 (ws). P to end of row.
Row 2 (rs). Bind off 3 (3) 2 sts, k to end of row.
Row 3. P to end of row.
Row 4. Bind off 2 sts, k to end of row.
Row 5. P to end of row.
Row 6. Bind off 1 st, k to end of row.
Work Rows 5–6 a total 2 (4) 3 times. Total 15 (15) 20 sts.
Now work even in pattern and stockinette until work measures 51 (54) 56cm [20 (21.25) 22in] from cast-on edge.
End with a k row and bind off.

Now replace the right shoulder sts on the needle.

Starting on the right (the knit) side, work these rows (continuing established pattern):
Row 1 (rs). K to end of row.
Row 2. Bind off 3 (3) 2 sts, p to end of row.
Row 3. K to end of row.
Row 4. Bind off 2 sts, p to end of row.
Row 5. K to end of row.
Row 6. Bind off 1 st, p to end of row.

Work Rows 5–6 a total 2 (4) 3 times.
15 (15) 20 sts remain.

Now work even in pattern and stockinette until work measures 51 (54) 56cm [20 (21.25) 22in] from cast-on edge. End with a p row and bind off.

Back
Replace back sts on needle and attach yarn from the right side of work. Continue in pattern.
Row 1 (rs). K to end of row.
Row 2. K1, p until 1 st remains, k1.

Now dec to shape the armholes:
Row 1 (rs). Bind off first st, k to end of row.
Row 2 (ws). Bind off first st, p until 1 st remains, k1.

Work Rows 1–2 total 10 (14) 17 times = 59 (66) 75 sts.

Now work even in pattern and stockinette until work measures 43 (45) 46cm [17 (17.75) 18in] from the cast-on edge. End with a p row.

Now bind off for the shoulder, while continuing in pattern:
Row 1 (rs). Bind off 3 (3) 4 sts, k to end of row.
Row 2. Bind off 3 (3) 4 sts, p until 1 st remains, k1.
Work Rows 1–2 total 5 times = 29 (36) 35 sts.

Bind off remaining sts.

Sewing the shoulders together:
Before sewing the shoulders together, work all loose ends into the reverse side of the slipover and trim off tails, so there are no loose strands. Sew the shoulder together with duplicate stitch.

Neck
Pick up and k76 (80) 84 sts along the neck opening with Colour A on 3.5mm (US 4) [UK 9 or 10] needles. Skip every 3rd loop on the vertical and diagonal edges, but pick up all sts on the horizontal edges. The total number of sts must be a multiple of 4.

Work 6 rnds of k2, p2 ribbing.

Work 2 rnds double-knit in k2, p2 ribbing.

Bind off with Italian bind-off.

Finishing the armholes:
Both armholes are finished identically. Pick up and knit about 76 (84) 88 sts around the armhole with Colour A on 3.5mm (US 4) [UK 9 or 10] needles. Skip every 3rd loop on vertical edges but pick up 1 st in each st on horizontal edges. The total number of sts must be a multiple of 4.

Work 6 rnds of k2, p2 ribbing.

Work 2 rnds double-knit in k2, p2 ribbing.

Bind off with Italian bind-off.

Finishing
Work all ends into the inside. You're done!

A long scarf that is knitted in the round

Bibi Scarf

Measurements
23 × 209cm [9 × 82.25 in]

Needles
Circular needle 2.5mm (US 1.5) [UK 12 or 13], 60cm [24in]
Circular needle 3.5mm (US 4) [UK 9 or 10], 60cm [24in]
If not using Magic Loop technique, use double-pointed needles in the same sizes.

Tapestry needle for finishing

Knitting Gauge/Tension
26 sts x 29 rnds on 3.5mm (US 4) [UK 9 or 10) needles in pattern with 2 yarns held together for each colour = 10 × 10cm (4 × 4in)

Yarns
2 strands of Ficolana's Saga yarn are held with 2 strands of Ficolana's Tilia yarn throughout. You can substitute Ficolana's Arwetta Classic for the Saga if you want a wider colour palette. In the scarf shown here, Arwetta was combined with Tilia for Colour F.

Colour A
Saga, Colour 302: 200g;
Tilia, Colour 321: 125g
Colour B
Saga, Colour 353: 50g
Tilia, Colour 353: 25g
Colour C
Saga, Colour 977: 50g
Tilia, Colour 101: 25g
Colour D
Saga, Colour 301: 50g
Tilia, Colour 340: 25g
Colour E
Saga, Colour 110: 100g
Tilia, Colour 325: 50g
Colour F
Arwetta, Colour 251: 50g
Tilia, Colour 196: 25g
Colour G
Saga, Colour 277: 50g
Tilia, Colour 218: 25g
Colour H
Saga, Colour 376: 50g
Tilia, Colour 279: 25g

Chart
Use Bibi chart in Pink on p. 53.

Scarf
Using Italian cast-on (k1, p1), cast on 104 sts on 2.5mm (US 1.5) [UK 12 or 13] needles needles 2 strands of with Colour A. Join into a rnd and place marker.

Work 2 rnds double-knit:
Rnd 1. *K1, sl 1 p-wise with yarn in front of needle. Rep from * to end of rnd.
Rnd 2 *Sl 1 p-wise with yarn in front, p1. Rep from * to end of rnd.

Change to k2, p2 ribbing.
Continue in ribbing until work measures 10cm [4in].

Change to 3.5mm (US 4) [UK 9 or 10] needles.
K 1 rnd, inc by make 1 rt at beg of rnd.
Total 105 sts.

Begin chart and rep the charted pattern 7 times in total to end of rnd.
Work rows 1–68 of Chart a total 9 times.
Then work Rows 1–21 of Chart again.

Change back to 2.5mm (US 1.5) [UK 12 or 13] needles and Colour A.
K 1 rnd, working k2tog at beg of rnd.
Total 104 sts.

Work 10cm [4in] in k2, p2 ribbing.
Work 2 rnds double-knit.
End with Italian bind off.

Finishing
Sew all ends into inside of tube. Wash according to yarn manufacturer's instructions. Stretch ribbing out to the width of the whole scarf. Lay the scarf flat on an absorbent surface to dry.

Mega Erika Jumper → 28

Icelandic
Hilda → 88

A striped sweater designed for Italian greyhounds and whippets

Stripe Overload for Sighthounds

Sizes
Iggy 1, (Iggy 2), Iggy 3,
(Whippet 1), Whippet 2, (Whippet 3)

Numbers refer to sizes of the two kinds of dogs.
1 = puppy
2 = medium
3 = large

Dog's Measurements
Back (from base of neck to base of tail):
33 (38) 43 (48) 53 (58)cm
[13 (15) 17 (19) 21 (23)in]
Girth (just behind shoulders):
35-40 (40-45) 45-50 (53-57)
57-61 (61-65)cm
[13.75–15.75 (15.75–17.75)
17.75–19.75 (21–22.5)in]

Needles
Circular needle 4mm (US 6) [UK 8],
40cm or 60cm [16 or 24in].
If not using Magic Loop technique, use double-pointed needles in the same size for 40cm (16in) circular.
Tapestry needle for finishing.

Knitting Gauge/Tension
17 sts x 27 rnds on 4mm (US 6) [UK 8] needles, with 2 yarns held together = 10 × 10cm (4 × 4in)

Yarns
Sandnes' Alpakka Ull held together with Ficolana's Tilia

Colour A
Alpakka Ull, Colour 6046 (Jolly Blue):
75 (75) 75 (100) 150 (150)g
Tilia, Colour 328 (Bluebell): 50 (50) 50 (50) 75 (75)g
Colour B
Alpakka Ull, Colour 9825 (Sunny Lime):
75 (75) 75 (100) 150 (150)g
Tilia, Colour 328 (French Vanilla):
50 (50) 50 (50) 75 (75)g

Info
These directions are designed specifically for sighthounds. If you want the directions for another breed, proceed to the next design, *Stripe Overload for Most Dogs* on p. 67.

The sweater is worked from neck to tail. It should fit snugly to begin with, as it will stretch some in use.

Raglan
Cast on 38 (42) 46 (50) 54 (58) sts with Colour A. Join into a round and place marker (Marker 4) at join.

Now place 3 additional markers:
K15 (17) 19 (21) 23 (25) sts across back, place Marker 1.
K7 (8) 8 (9) 9 (10) sts for right foreleg, place Marker 2.
K9 (9) 11 (11) 13 (13) sts across breast, place Marker 3.
K7 (8) 8 (9) 9 (10) sts to end of rnd.
Marker 4 is already in place.

Inc every 2nd rnd on the back and every 4th rnd on the foreleg markers. Do not inc in the breast area at this point.
At the same time, work the stripe pattern alternating 2 rnds of A and 2 of B. Change now to B.

Rnd 1. (Inc for back and forelegs) K1, make 1 left, k to 1 st before Marker 1 (back), make 1 rt, k2, make 1 left, k to 1 st before Marker 2 (rt foreleg), make 1 rt, k (across breast) to Marker 3 (left shoulder), k1, make 1 left, k to 1 st before Marker 4, make 1 rt, k1.
Rnd 2. K to end of rnd.
Rnd 3. (Inc for back only) K1, make 1 left, k to 1 st before Marker 1, k1, make 1 rt, k to end of rnd.
Rnd 4. K to end of rnd.

Work Rnds 1–4 a total 3 (4) 4 (5) 6 (7) times.
62 (74) 78 (90) 102 (114) sts.

Now work 4 more rnds where you also inc on the breast section:

Rnd 1. (Inc for back, forelegs and breast section) K1, make 1 left, k to 1 st before Marker 1, make 1 right, k2, make 1 left, k to 1 st before Marker 2, make 1 rt, k2, make 1 left, k to 1 st before Marker 3, make 1 rt, k2, make 1 left, k to 1 st before Marker 4, make 1 rt, k1.

Rnd 2. K to end of rn.
Rnd 3. K1, make 1 left, k to 1 st before Marker 1, make 1 rt, k1, k to Marker 2, k1, make 1 left, k to 1 st before Marker 3, make 1 rt, k to Marker 4.
Rnd 4. K to end of rnd.
Total 74 (86) 90 (102) 114 (126) sts.

Now divide the sts into groups:
31 (37) 39 (45) 51 (57) sts for the back, 15 (18) 18 (21) 23 (26) sts for each foreleg and 13 (13) 15 (15) 17 (17) sts for the breast.

Next rnd. (Remove Markers 1–3 as you go.) K to Marker 1, place the rt foreleg 15 (18) 18 (21) 23 (26) sts on a holder. Cast on 7 (8) 8 (9) 9 (10) sts over the gap, k to next marker, place the left foreleg 15 (18) 18 (21) 23 (26) sts on a holder, and cast on 7 (8) 8 (9) 9 (10) sts over the gap. Make a new rnd of these sts and leave Marker 4 in place as the beg of the rnd. Total 58 (66) 70 (78) 86 (94) sts for the body.

Body
In the first rnd, place a new marker: k to the newly cast on sts under the rt foreleg, place marker, k to end of rnd.

Now work ribbing on the underside of the body and continue working stockinette on the back:
Next rnd. K to marker, then *k1, p1. Rep from * until 1 st remains in the rnd, p1.

Rep this rnd until the ribbed portion measures 8 (10) 14 (16) 18 (21)cm [3.25 (4) 5.5 (6.25) 7 (8.25)in] or reaches the point where the dog's belly meets the base of the ribcage.

Finish whichever colour stripe is in progress and work 1 rnd in the next colour.

Now bind off for the belly:
Next rnd: K across the back sts, placing a marker at the centermost st of the back. K to marker, work 6 sts ribbing following the existing ribs, bind off in ribbing until 6 sts remain in the rnd, then work 6 sts ribbing.

Break both yarns, remove the beg-of-rnd marker and slip the 6 sts on the rt needle onto the left. Now work back and forth instead of circularly, while both decreasing and increasing. Keep on striping!

Row 1 (rs). Sl 1 p-wise, work 5 sts ribbing, make 1 left, K to 3 sts before marker, k2tog left, k3, k2tog, k until 6 sts remain in row, make 1 rt, rib 6 sts.
Row 2 (ws) Sl 1 p-wise, work 5 sts ribbing, p across until 6 sts remain, work 5 sts ribbing, k1.
Row 3. Sl 1 p-wise, work 5 sts ribbing, then k until 6 sts remain, rib 6 sts.
Row 4. Rep Row 2.
Row 5. Sl 1 p-wise, work 5 sts ribbing, k until 3 sts before marker, k2tog Left, k3, k2tog, k until 6 sts remain in row, work 6 sts ribbing.
Row 6. Rep Row 2.
Row 7. Rep Row 3.
Row 8. Rep Row 2.

Work Rows 1–8 a total 4 (4) 4 (4) 5 (5) times.

Work 4 rows ribbing:
Row 1 (rs). Sl 1 p-wise, *p1, k1. Rep from * to end of row.
Row 2 (ws). Sl 1 p-wise, *k1, p1. Rep from * until 2 sts remain, k2.

Work 2 rows double-knit:
Row 1 (rs). Sl 1 p-wise, *p1, sl 1 p-wise with yarn behind needle. Rep from * until 2 sts remain, p1, k1.
Row 2 (ws). Sl 1 p-wise, *sl 1 p-wise with yarn behind needle, p1. Rep from * until 2 sts remain, sl 1 k st with yarn behind needle, k1.

Bind off with Italian bind off.

Forelegs
Place the sts for one foreleg on 4mm (US 6) [UK 8] dp needles. Starting in the middle of the cast-on sts, pick up and k3 (4) 4 (4) 4 (5) sts, k the shoulder sts and pick up the last 4 (4) 4 (5) 5 (5) cast-on sts, join in a rnd and place marker.

Work around in stockinette, with decs every 10th (11th) 11th (11th) 11th (11th) rnd 3 (3) 3 (4) 4 (5) times: K1, k2tog, k until 3 sts remain in rnd, k2tog left, k1. End with a stripe in Colour A.

Dogs' legs can be quite different in length. You can also knit until the sweater leg is approx 2cm (just under an inch) above your dog's dew claw. K 1 rnd with B, and then work 4 rnds k1, p1 ribbing.

Work 2 rnds of double-knit:
Rnd 1. *K1, sl 1 p-wise with yarn in front of work. Rep from * to end of rnd.
Rnd 2. *sl 1 st p-wise with yarn behind work, p1. Rep from * to end of rnd.

End with Italian bind-off.

Make the second leg in the same way.

Turtleneck
Pick up and k38 (42) 46 (50) 54 (58) sts on 4mm (US 6) [UK 8] dp needles along the neckline, join into a round and place marker. Work even up in k1, p1 ribbing until turtleneck measures about 8.25 (8.75) 10.25 (11.75) 11.5 (13.5)in] [21 (22) 26 (30) 32 (34)cm. End with a stripe in Colour B.

Work 2 rnds double-knit as described above under forelegs.

End with Italian bind-off.

Finishing
With tapestry needle, work all loose yarn tails into wrong side of garment.

Stripe Overload for Most Dogs

Sizes
1 (2) 3 (4) 5 (6)

1 Chihuahua
(2 Coton de Tulear, Shih Tzu)
3 Jack Russell Terrier, Pug
(4 French Bulldog, Beagle)
5 Collie, Labradoodle
(6 Golden Retriever)

Dog's Measurements
Back (from base of neck to base of tail):
25-30 (30-36) 35-42 (42-48)
48-55 (54-62)cm
[10–12 (12–14) 13.75–16.5 (16.5–19)
19–21.75 (21.25–24.5) in]

Needles
Circular needle 4mm (US 6) [UK 8], 60cm [24in].
If not using Magic Loop technique use double-pointed needles in the same size.

Knitting Gauge/Tension
17 sts and 27 rows on 4mm (US 6) [UK 8] needles = 10 × 10cm (4 × 4 in)

Yarn
Sandnes' Alpakka Ull
Main colour (MC) 6046 (Jolly Blue):
50 (50) 100 (150) 200 (200)g
Contrast colour (CC) 9825 (Sunny Lime):
50 (50) 100 (150) 200 (200)g

Info
These directions are designed for various breeds of dog; however, if you want to knit for a greyhound or whippet, use the preceding pattern on p. 65.

The sweater is worked from neckline to tail. It should be rather tight to start with but will loosen up in use.

A selvage- or edge-stitch is worked by slipping the first st purlwise with the yarn in front of the needle. In the next row, from the wrong side, the same st is knitted.

Neck Opening and Raglan
Cast on 38 (42) 50 (58) 70 (76) sts on 4mm (US 6) [UK 8] needle and MC. Join to knit circularly a place a marker for beg of rnd (Marker 4).

Place 3 more markers:
K15 (17) 19 (21) 25 (27) sts across back, place Marker 1.
K7 (8) 10 (12) 15 (16) sts for right foreleg, place Marker 2.
K9 (9) 11 (13) 15 (17) sts across breast, place Marker 3.
K7 (8) 10 (12) 15 (16) sts for left foreleg. Marker 4 is already in place.

You will increase every 2nd rnd on the back and every 4 rnd on the forelegs. There are no increases on the breast section at this point. At the same time, you will knit stripes, alternating 2 rnds of MC and 2 rnds CC. Change now to CC.

Rnd 1. (Incs on back and forelegs) K1, make 1 left, k to 1 st before Marker 1, make 1 right, k2, make 1 left, k to 1 st before Marker 2, make 1 rt, k1, k to Marker 3, k1, make 1 left, k to 1 st before Marker 4, m 1 right, k1.
Rnd 2. Kto end of rnd.
Rnd 3. (Incs on back only) K1, make 1 left, k to 1 st before Marker 1, make 1 right, and k rest of rnd.
Rnd 4. K to end of rnd.

Work Rnds 1–4 a total 3 (4) 5 (6) 7 (8) times = 62 (74) 90 (106) 126 (140) sts.

Now knit 4 more rnds, where there are also incs on the breast section:
Rnd 1. (Inc for back, forelegs and breast section) k1, make 1 left, k until 1 st before Marker 1, make 1 rt, k2, make 1 left, k until 1 st before Marker 2, make 1 rt, k2, make 1 left, k until 1 st before Marker 3, make 1 rt, k2, make 1 left, k until 1 st before Marker 4, make 1 rt, k1.
Rnd 2. K to end of rnd.
Rnd 3. K1, make 1 left, k to 1 st before Marker 1, make 1 right, k1, k to Marker 2, k1, make 1 left, k to 1 st before Marker 3, make 1 right, k1, k to Marker 4.
Rnd 4. K to end of rnd.
Total 74 (86) 102 (118) 138 (152) sts.

Divide the sts into sections:
31 (37) 43 (49) 57 (63) sts across the back,
15 (18) 22 (26) 31 (34) sts for right foreleg.
13 (13) 15 (17) 19 (21) sts for breast section.
15 (18) 22 (26) 31 (34) sts for left foreleg.

Next rnd: Remove markers as you work, except Marker 4, beg of rnd. K to Marker 1 and put right foreleg sts on a st holder, and cast on 6 (7) 8 (10) 11 (12) sts, k to Marker 2, put left foreleg sts on a st holder and cast on 6 (7) 8 (10) 11 (12) sts, join into a new rnd, leaving Marker 4 in place as beg of rnd. Total 56 (64) 74 (86) 98 (108) sts for body of sweater.

Body
On the first rnd, k to the newly cast-on sts by the right foreleg and set marker, then k to end of rnd.

Now work ribbing on the belly side of the body piece, but continue with stockinette on the back.

Next rnd: K to the marker, then work p1, k1 ribbing until 1 st remains, p1.

Rep this rnd until the ribbed portion measures 9 (10) 12 (15) 20 (25)cm [3.5 (4) 4.75 (6) 8 (10.75)in], or until the point where the dog's belly meets his stomach.

Finish whichever colour stripe is in progress and work rnd in the next colour.

Now bind off for the belly:
K15 (18) 21 (24) 28 (31) sts, place a marker at the centre st of the back section (marking the dec line), k to marker, k6 sts ribbing, bind off in ribbing until 6 sts remain in rnd, rib to end of rnd. Total 43 (49) 55 (61) 69 (75) sts.

Now work the final part of the back: Break both MC and CC, remove the rnd marker and move the 6 sts on the right needle onto the left. You'll be knitting back and forth now instead of around, while making decs and incs. Continue striping.

Row 1 (rs). Sl 1 p-wise, k5 sts ribbing, make 1 left, k to 3 sts before marker, k2tog left, k3, k2tog, k even until 6

sts remain in row, make 1 right, k6.
Row 2. Sl 1 p-wise, rib 5 sts, purl until 6 sts remain, rib 6 sts.
Row 3. Sl 1 p-wise, rib 5 sts, k even until 6 sts remain, rib 6 sts.
Row 4. Rep Row 2.
Row 5. Sl 1 p-wise, rib 5 sts, k until 3 sts before marker, k2tog left, k3, k2tog, k until 6 sts remain, rib 6 sts.
Row 6. Rep Row 2.
Row 7. Rep Row 3.
Row 8. Rep Row 2.

Work Rows 1–8 a total 4 (4) 4 (4) 5 (5) times = 35 (41) 47 (53) 61 (67) sts.

Work 4 rows of ribbing as follows:
Row 1 (rs). Sl 1 p-wise, *p1, k1. Rep from * to end of row.
Row 2. Sl 1 p-wise, *k1, p1. Rep from * until 2 sts remain, k2.
Repeat both rows once.

K2 rows of double-knit:
Row 1 (rs). Sl 1 p-wise, *p1, sl 1 p-wise with yarn behind work. Rep from * until 2 sts remain, p1, k1.
Row 2. Sl 1 p-wise, *Sl 1 p-wise with yarn behind work, p1, and rep until 2 sts remain, sl 1 k-wise with yarn behind work, k1.

End with Italian bind-off.

Forelegs
Replace one foreleg section back on needles. Pick up and k3 (4) 4 (5) 5 (6) sts starting at the middle of the cast-on sts, k the foreleg sts and finally pick up and knit the final 4 (4) 4 (5) 6 (6) cast-on sts, join for circular knitting and place a marker. Total 22 (26) 30 (36) 42 (46) sts.

Work in stockinette while decreasing every 6th (6th) 7th (7th) 8th (8th) rnd a total 3 (3) 4 (4) 5 (5) times: K1, k2tog, k until 3 sts before marker, k2tog left, k1. 16 (20) 22 (28) 32 (36) sts.

End with a stripe in MC.

Dogs' legs can be quite different in length. You can also knit until the sweater leg is approx 2cm (just under an inch) above your dog's dew claw.

K 1 rnd with CC and then work 4 rnds k1, p1 ribbing. Keep striping!

Work 2 rnds double-knitting as described for end of the back section,
End with Italian bind-off.

Work the second foreleg following the directions above.

Neck
Pick up and k38 (42) 50 (58) 70 (76) sts around the neck opening, join into a rnd and place marker.
Work even in k1, p1 ribbing until neck edging measures 18 (20) 22 (24) 26 (28)cm [7 (8) 8.5 (9.5) 10.25 (11)in].
End with a stripe in CC.

Work 2 rnds double-knit.
End with Italian bind-off.

Finishing
Use a tapestry needle to work all ends into the ws of the knit.

A faux-fur sweater specially for Italian greyhounds and whippets

Fat Fur Sweater for Sighthounds

Sizes
Iggy 1, (Iggy 2), Iggy 3
(Whippet 1), Whippet 2, (Whippet 3)

1 = puppy
2 = medium
3 = large

Dog's Measurements
Back (from base of neck to base of tail):
33 (38) 43 (48) 53 (58)cm
[13 (15) 17 (19) 20.8 (22.8)in]
Girth behind shoulders:
35-40 (40-45) 45-50 (53-57) 57-61 (61-65)cm
[13.75–15.75 (15.75–17.75) 17.75–19.75 (21–22.5) 22.5–24 (24–25.5)in]

Needles
Circular needle 6mm (US 10) [UK 4], 60cm [24in]
Circular needle 4mm (US 6) [UK 8], 60cm [24in].
If not using Magic Loop technique, use double-pointed needles in the same sizes.
Tapestry needle for finishing.

Knitting Gauge/Tension
14 sts x 23 rows on 6mm (US 10) [UK 4] needles with 2 strands held together = 10 × 10cm (4 × 4in)

Yarns
Permin's Bella
Pink version: Colour 883264 (Sart Rose)
or
Green version: 883274 (Salvia)
100 (100) 150 (200) 200 (200)g

Other equipment
Mohair brush

Info
These directions are designed specifically for sighthounds. If you want the directions for another breed, proceed to the next design, *Fat Fur Sweater for Most Dogs* on p. 73.

The sweater is worked from neckline to tail with 2 strands held together. It should fit snugly to start with but will loosen up in use.

A selvage- or edge-stitch is worked by slipping the first st purlwise with the yarn in front of the needle. In the next row, from the wrong side, the same st is knitted.

Raglan
Cast on 26 (30) 34 (36) 40 (44) sts on 6mm (US 10) [UK 4] needles with both yarns held together. Join into a rnd and place marker.

Now place 3 additional markers:
K11 (13) 15 (15) 17 (19) sts across back, place Marker 1 (inc point for right back).
K5 (5) 6 (7) 7 (8) sts for right foreleg, place Marker 2 (inc point for breast).
K5 (7) 7 (7) 9 (9) sts across breast, place Marker 3.
K5 (5) 6 (7) 7 (8) sts for left foreleg and to end of rnd and Marker 4, (inc point for left back and beg of rnd).

Inc every 2nd rnd on the back and every 4th rnd on the foreleg markers. Do not inc in the breast area at this point:
Rnd 1. (Incs on back and forelegs) K1, make 1 left, k to 1 st before Marker 1, make 1 rt, k2, make 1 left, k to 1 st before Marker 2, make 1 rt, k1, k to Marker 3, k1 make 1 left, k to 1 st before Marker 4, make 1 rt, k1.
Rnd 2. K to end of rnd.
Rnd 3. (Inc on back only) K1, make 1 left, k to 1 st before Marker 1, make 1 rt, k to end of rnd.
Rnd 4. K to end of rnd.

Work Rnds 1–4 a total 4 (5) 5 (6) 7 (7) times.

Sizes Iggy 3 (Whippet 3) only:
Work Rnds 1–2 again.
Total 58 (70) 74 (84) 96 (100) sts.

Divide the sts into sections, starting at Marker 4:
27 (33) 35 (39) 45 (47) sts for back,
13 (15) 17 (19) 21 (23) sts for right foreleg,
5 (7) 8 (7) 9 (10) sts for breast section,
13 (15) 17 (19) 21 (23) sts for left foreleg.

Next rnd. K to Marker 1 (leave marker in place), place right foreleg sts on a holder, cast on 5 (5) 7 (9) 9 (11) sts, remove Marker 2, k to Marker 3 and remove it, place left foreleg sts on a holder and cast on 5 (5) 7 (9) 9 (11) sts, join once more into a rnd and leave Marker 4 in place for beg of rnd. Total 42 (50) 56 (64) 72 (82) sts.

Body

The belly portion will be ribbed now, while the back section continues in stockinette:

Next rnd. K to marker, *p1, k1. Rep from * until 1 st remains in rnd, p1. Rep this rnd until the ribbing portion measures 4 (5) 6 (8) 8 (9)cm [1.5 (2) 2.25 (3.25) 3.25 (3.5)in].

Now work short rows to shape back. I recommend the German Short Rows method.

Rnd 1. K to 4 sts before marker, turn.
P to 4 sts before marker, turn.
K to 4 sts before marker, turn.
K to end of rnd, and rib as before.
Rnds 2–6. K and rib to end of rnd as before.
Rnd 7. Rep Rnd 1.
Rnds 8–11. K and rib to end of rnd as before.
Rnd 12. K to marker and bind off in ribbing.

Now work back and forth now instead of around.

Row 1 (rs). Sl 1 p-wise, p1, k1, p1, then k until 4 sts remain, turn; (ws) p until 4 sts remain in row, turn; (rs) k until 4 sts remain in row, turn; p1, k1, p1, k1.
Row 2 (ws). Sl 1 p-wise, k1, p1, k1, p until 4 sts remain in row, k1, p1, k2.
Row 3. Sl 1 p-wise, p1, k1, p1, k until 4 sts remain in row, p1, k1, p1, k1.
Row 4. Rep Row 2.
Row 5. Rep Row 3.
Row 6. Rep Row 2.

Rep these 6 rows 0 (0) 0 (0) 1 (1) time. On the final row, place a marker (ctr marker) on the centermost st of the last row to mark dec point.

Now dec across the back while also working more short rows:
Row 1. Sl 1 p-wise, p1, k1, p1, k until 3 sts before the ctr marker, k2tog left, k3, k2tog, k until 4 sts remain in row, turn.
P until 4 sts remain on needle, turn.
K until 4 sts remain on needle, p1, k1, p1, k1.
Row 2. Sl 1 p-wise, k1, p1, k1, p until 4 sts remain in row, k1, p1, k2.
Row 3. Sl 1 p-wise, p1, k1, p1, k until 3 sts before ctr marker, k2tog left, k3, k2tog, and k until 4 sts remain in row, p1, k1, p1, k1.
Row 4. Rep Row 2.
Row 5. Sl 1 p-wise, p1, k1, p1 and k until 4 sts remain in row, p1, k1, p1, k1.
Row 6 Rep Row 2.
Work Rows 1–6 again, then work Rows 1–2.

Now work ribbing:
Row 1. Sl 1 p-wise, *p1, k1. Rep from * to end of row.
Row 2. Sl 1 p-wise, *k1, p1. Rep from * until 2 sts remain in row, k2.
Row 3. Rep Row 1.
Bind off in ribbing.

Forelegs

Place one set of foreleg sts back on 6mm (US 10) [UK 4] needle. Starting in the middle of the cast-on sts, k2 (2) 3 (4) 4 (5) sts, k the foreleg section, and finally k the last 3 (3) 4 (5) 5 (6) cast-on sts; join as a rnd and place marker.

Work in stockinette and dec every 6th (6th) 6th (7th) 7th (7th) rnd: K1, k2tog, and k until 3 sts remain in rnd, k2tog left, k1. Work this dec rnd 3 (3) 4 (4) 5 (5) times.

Now knit 5 (5) 5 (6) 6 (6) rnds stockinette.

Dogs' legs can be quite different in length. You can also knit until the sweater leg is approx 2cm (just under an inch) above your dog's dew claw.

Work 3 rnds of k1, p1 ribbing and bind off.

Neck

With 4mm (US 6) [UK 8] needle, pick up and k26 (30) 34 (36) 40 (44) sts along the neck edge, join as rnd and place marker.
K even in k1, p1 ribbing until neckband measures 23 (25) 27 (29) 30 (32)cm [9 (10) 10.75 (11.5) 24 (24.5)in].

Bind off in ribbing.

Finishing

With tapestry needle, work all ends into wrong side of work.
Wash the sweater following yarn manufacturer's instructions.
Lay it out flat to dry. Fluff up the fibres with the mohair brush starting at the neck and working down. Brush small sections at a time.

Fat Fur Sweater for Most Dogs

Sizes
1 (2) 3 (4) 5 (6)

1 = Chihuahua
2 = Coton de Tulear, Shih Tzu
3 = Jack Russell Terrier, Pug
4 = French Bulldog, Beagle
5 = Collie, Labradoodle
6 = Golden Retriever

Dog's Measurements
Back (from base of neck to base of tail):
25-30 (30-36) 35-42 (42-48)
48-55 (54-62)cm
[10–12 (12–14) 13.75–16.5 (16.5–19)
19–21.75 (21.25–24.5)in]

Needles
Circular needle 6mm (US 10)
[UK 4], 60cm [24in]
Circular needle 4mm (US 6)
[UK 8], 60cm [24in].
If not using Magic Loop technique, use double-pointed needles in the same sizes.
Tapestry needle for finishing.

Knitting Gauge/Tension
14 sts x 23 rows on 6mm (US 10) [UK 4] needles
with 2 strands held together
= 10 × 10cm (4 × 4in).

Yarns
Permin's Bella
Pink version: Colour 883264 (Sart Rosa)
or
Green version: Colour 883274 (Salvie)
100 (100) 150 (200) 250 (300)g

Other tools
Mohair brush

Info
These directions are designed for various breeds of dog; however, if you want to knit for a greyhound or whippet, use the preceding pattern on p. 65.

The sweater is worked from the neck down. It should fit tightly to start with, as it will stretch somewhat in use.

A selvage- or edge-stitch is worked by slipping the first st purlwise with the yarn in front of the needle. In the next row, from the wrong side, the same st is knitted.

Raglan
Cast on 30 (32) 36 (38) 40 (44) sts on 6mm (US 10) [UK 4] needle with 2 strands of yarn held together.
Join into rnd and place marker (Marker 4).

Add 3 more markers: K13 (13) 15 (17) 17 (19) (across the back),
Place Marker 1.
K6 (7) 7 (7) 8 (8) (beg of right foreleg),
Place Marker 2.
K5 (5) 7 (7) 7 (9) (beg of breast, end of foreleg),
Place Marker 3.
K6 (7) 7 (7) 8 (8) (end of breast, beg of left foreleg).

Inc every 2nd rnd on the back section and every 4th rnd for the forelegs. There are no incs at this point for the breast section:

Rnd 1. (Inc for both back and forelegs): K1, make 1 left, k to 1 st before Marker 1, make 1 rt, k2, make 1 left, k to 1 st before Marker 2, make 1 rt, k1, k to Marker 3, k1, make 1 left, k to 1 st before Marker 4, make 1 rt, k1.
Rnd 2. Knit to end of rnd.
Rnd 3. (Inc for back) K1, make 1 left, k to 1 st before marker 1, make 1 rt, k rest of rnd.
Rnd 4. Knit to end of rnd.

Work Rnds 1–4 a total 3 (4) 5 (6) 7 (8) times.
Work Rnd 1 once more.
Total 60 (70) 82 (92) 102 (114) sts.

Divide the sts into sections:
27 (31) 37 (43) 47 (53) sts for the back,
14 (17) 19 (21) 24 (26) sts for rt foreleg
5 (5) 7 (7) 7 (9) sts for breast portion,
14 (17) 19 (21) 24 (26) sts for left foreleg.

Next round. K to Marker 1 (let it stay in place), place right foreleg sts on a holder and cast on 4 (5) 7 (7) 7 (8) sts, remove Marker 2, k to Marker 3, remove Marker 3 and set the left foreleg sts on a holder and cast on 4 (5) 7 (7) 7 (8) sts, and rejoin sts into a round. Leave Marker 4, the beg of the rnd, in place. Total 40 (46) 58 (64) 68 (78) sts.

Body

Now work ribbing on the belly side of the body, and continue stockinette on the back:

Next rnd. K to Marker 1, *p1, k1.
Rep from * until 1 st remains in rnd, p1.
Rep this rnd until the rib portion measures 9 (10) 11 (12) 13 (14)cm [3.5 (4) 4.25 (4.75) 5.125 (5.5)in] or to where the dog's chest begins to round into a belly.
Next rnd. K to marker and bind off the ribbing sts.

You will now knit back and forth instead of circularly.

Row 1 (rs). Sl 1 p-wise, p1, k1, p1, k until 4 sts remain in the row, p1, k1, p1, k1.
Row 2 (ws). Sl 1 p-wise, k1, p1, k1, then p until 4 sts remain, k1, p1, k1.
Work Rows 1–2 a total 5 (6) 7 (7) 8 (8) times, then place a marker on the centermost st of the last row.

Now decrease on the back:
Row 1. Sl 1 p-wise, p1, k1, p1, k to 3 sts before the centre back marker, k2tog left, k3, k2tog, then k until 4 sts remain in row, p1, k1, p1, k1.
Row 2. Sl 1 p-wise, k1, p1, k1, p until 4 sts remain , k1, p1, k2.
Row 3. Sl 1 p-wise, p1, k1, p1, k until 4 sts remain, p1, k1, p1, k1.
Row 4. Repeat Row 2.

Work Rows 1–4 another 1 (1) 1 (2) 2 (3) times.

Now work ribbing:
Row 1. Sl 1 p-wise, *p1, k1. Rep from * to end of row.
Row 2. Sl 1 p-wise, *k1, p1. Rep from * until 2 sts remain, k2.
Row 3. Rep Row 1.

Bind off in ribbing.

Forelegs

Put the sts for 1 foreleg back on 6mm (US 10) [UK 4] needle. Starting from the middle of the cast-on sts, pick up and k2 (3) 4 (4) 4 (4) cast-on sts, k the foreleg section and pick up and k the remaining 2 (2) 3 (3) 3 (4) cast-on sts. Join into a rnd and place a marker for beg of rnd. Total 18 (22) 26 (28) 31 (34) sts.

Work in stockinette while making decs every 3rd (4th) 4th (5th) 5th (6th) rnd a total 4 (4) 5 (5) 6 (6) times. At beg of dec rnd: k1, k2tog, k until 3 sts before marker, tw k2tog left, k1.

Dogs' legs can be quite different in length. You can also knit until the sweater leg is approx 2cm (just under an inch) above your dog's dew claw.

Work 3 rnds k1, p1 ribbing. Bind off.

Make the other sweater leg following the same directions.

Neck

Pick up and k30 (32) 36 (38) 40 (44) sts on 4mm (US 6) [UK 8] needles, join into a rnd and place a marker. Work even in k1, p1 ribbing until neck band measures 10 (11) 12 (14) 16 (18) cm [4 (4.25) 4.75 (5.5) 6.25 (7)in].

Bind off loosely in k1, p1 ribbing.

Finishing

With a tapestry needle, work in all loose ends on the wrong side.

Wash sweater following the manufacturer's instructions for yarn.

Lay flat to dry. With a mohair brush, fluff and brush the fibres from the neck downward. Take small sections at a time.

Stripe Overload Polo

Sizes
XS (S) M (L) XL (XXL)

Measurements
Chest: 101 (106) 111 (116) 122 (128)cm
[39.75 (41.75) 43.75 (45.75) 48 (50.5)in]
Length: 48 (49) 51 (53) 54 (56)cm
[19 (19.25) 20 9 (21.75) 21.25 (22)in]

Needles
Circular needle 4mm (US 6)
[UK 8], 60cm [24in]
Circular needle 5mm (US 8)
[UK 6], 80cm [32in]
If not using Magic Loop technique use double-pointed needles in the same sizes.
Tapestry needle for finishing.

Knitting Gauge/Tension
16 sts x 24 rows on 5mm (US 8) [UK 6] needles in stockinette with two yarns held together throughout = 10 × 10cm (4 × 4in)

Yarns
Colour A:
Sandnes' Alpakka Ull
Colour 6046 (Jolly Blue):
200 (250) 250 (300) 300 (350)g
Filcolana's Tilia
Colour 328 (Bluebell)
50 (50) 50 (75) 75 (100)g
Colour B
Sandnes' Alpakka Ull
Colour 9825 (Sunny Lime):
200 (250) 250 (300) 300 (350)g
Filcolana's Tilia
Colour 196 (French Vanilla)
50 (50) 50 (75) 75 (100)g

Info
The polo is worked from the top down in one piece.

A selvage- or edge-stitch is worked by slipping the first st purlwise with the yarn in front of the needle. In the next row, from the wrong side, the same st is knitted.

Collar
Cast on 103 (103) 107 (107) 111 (111) sts on 4mm (US 6) [UK 8] needles, with Colour A, using Italian cast-on (start with knit) then work 2 rows double-knit:
Row 1. *Sl 1 p-wise with yarn in front of needle, k1. Rep from * until 1 st remains, sl 1 p-wise with yarn in front.
Row 2. *K1, sl 1 p-wise with yarn in front. Rep from * until 1 st remains, k1.
Next row. Sl 1 st p-wise, *k1, p1; rep from * until 2 sts remain, k2.

Now change to Colour B and from here on alternate 2 rows of each colour. Don't break the yarn when changing colour and be careful not to pull the new colour tight when starting a new stripe. The purl side of the collar is the side that will be visible on the finished sweater.

Row 1 (ws). Sl 1 p-wise, *p1, k1. Rep from * to end of row.
Row 2 (rs). Sl 1 p-wise, *k1, p1. Rep from * until 2 sts rem, k2.
Row 3. Rep Row 1.
Row 4. Rep Row 2.
Row 5. Rep Row 1.
Row 6. Sl 1 p-wise, *k1, p1, dbl dec right, work ribbing until 6 sts remain, dbl dec left, work ribbing until 2 sts remain, k2.

Work Rows 1–6 a total 4 times, then rib for 5 more rows.
Total 87 (87) 91 (91) 95 (95) sts.

Break both colours and turn work as if to work Row 6.

Move the first 28 (28) 30 (30) 32 (32) 32 over to the right needle, place a marker (beg of rnd), and attach Colour B again. Rib to end of needle (following existing ribbing) until 2 sts remain, k2tog left, cast on 1 st, join into a rnd and k the next 2 sts tog (the 2 first 2 sts from the opposite side of the collar), and work ribbing to marker. Work 1 rnd in ribbing. Total 86 (86) 90 (90) 94 (94) 94 sts.

An oversized polo sweater with stripes

Now place markers to divide the work into back, sleeve, front, and sleeve. The beg-of-rnd marker is between the right sleeve and the back. Optionally, use a different colour or type marker, so you can easily tell the rnd marker apart from the others.

Next rnd. Rib 30 (30) 31 (31) 32 (32) sts (back), place marker.
Rib 13 (13) 14 (14) 15 (15) sts (sleeve), place marker.
Rib 30 (30) 31 (31) 32 (32) sts (front), place marker.
Rib 13 (13) 14 (14) 15 (15) sts (sleeve) to beg of rnd marker.

Raglan shoulders
Change to 5mm (US 8) [UK 6] needles and now work around in stockinette (always k sts). K2 rnds.

Now work short rows back and forth to shape the back neckline, while starting incs for the raglan shoulders. Use German Short Rows:
Row 1 (rs). K1, make 1 left, *k to 1 st before marker, make 1 rt,* k2, make 1 left. Rep from * to * once more, k2, turn.
Row 2 (ws). P to start of rnd, p1, p-make 1 rt, p to 1 st before marker, p-make 1 left, p2, make 1 p-wise rt, turn.
K to beg of rnd.

Work Rows 1–2 total 4 times, but each time turn 2 sts beyond the preceding turn, so that you knit the last turn st and 1 st after and then turn. In this way, the short rows reach farther and farther toward the middle of the front section. Remember to change colours to for the stripes.

You've now increased for the raglan 4 times. Go back to working circularly again on the rt side. Total 118 (118) 122 (122) 126 (126) sts.

Continue the raglan incs:
Rnd 1. (Inc) K1, make 1 left, *k to 1 st before marker, make 1 rt, k2, make 1 left. Rep from * 3 more times, then k to 1 st before marker, make 1 rt, k1.
Rnd 2. K the whole rnd even.

Work these 2 rnds a total 17 (19) 21 (23) 24 (26) times. You've now increased 21 (23) 25 (27) 28 (30) times for a total 254 (270) 290 (306) 318 (334) sts.

The sts are distributed as:
72 (76) 81 (85) 88 (92) sts each for front and back sections and 55 (59) 64 (68) 71 (75) sts for each sleeve.

Body
Divide the work into body and sleeve sections, removing markers as you go:
K across the back sts, place the rt sleeve sts on a holder, cast on 8 (8) 8 (8) 10 (10) sts (right underarm) and k across the sts for the front, place the sts for the left sleeve sts on a holder, and cast on 8 (8) 8 (8) 10 (10) sts (left underarm) and place the beg of rnd marker after the 4th (4th) 4th (4th) 5th (5th) st. Total 160 (168) 178 (186) 196 (204) sts for the body.

Continue in stockinette until work measures 42 (43) 45 (47) 48 (50)cm [16.5 (17) 17.75 (18.5) 19 (19.75)in] measured from the back of the neck (minus the collar), or 6cm [2.5in] less than your desired length. End with a stripe in Colour B.

Change back to 4mm (US 6) [UK 8] needles, and k 1 rnd, then work 12 rnds k1, p1 ribbing. The last part of the ribbing is a Colour A stripe; the double-knit and bind-off are in Colour B.

Work 2 rnds double-knit:

Rnd 1. *K1, sl 1 p-wise with yarn in front of work. Rep from * to end of rnd.
Rnd 2. *Sl 1 p-wise with yarn behind work, p1 and rep from * to end of rnd. End with Italian bind-off.

Sleeves
Put the sts for one sleeve back on around needles. Pick up and k8 (8) 8 (8) 10 (10) sts of the sts cast on for the underarm placing a marker after the 4th (4th) 4th (4th) 5th (5th) sts for beg of rnd. Total 63 (67) 72 (76) 81 (85) sts.

Continue in stripes and stockinette. Dec every 12th (12th) 11th (11th) 10th (10th) rnd 8 (8) 9 (9) 10 (10) 11 times: K1, k2tog, k until 3 sts remain in rnd, k2tog left, k1 for a total of 47 (51) 54 (58) 61 (65) sts.

K even from here in stockinette until sleeve measures 40 (40) 41 (42) 42 (43) cm [15.75 (15.75) 16.125 (16.5) 16.5 (17)in], measured along the inner arm (dec line) or until sleeve is 6cm [2.5in] shorter than your desired length. Finish the stripe in progress.

Change back to 4mm (US 6) [UK 8] needles. K 1 rnd, decreasing 5 (5) 6 (8) 9 (9) sts by working k2tog evenly spaced around. Total 42 (46) 48 (50) 52 (56) sts.

Work the cuff ribbing the same way as the ribbing on the body. Make a matching sleeve following these directions.

Finishing.
With a tapestry needle, work all ends into sts on the reverse side.

An oversized pullover in a patterned knit

Hilda Oversize Slipover

Sizes
XS-S (M) L (XL) XXL

Measurements
Chest: 102 (114) 125 (137) 148cm
[40 (44.75) 49.25 (54) 58.25in]
Length: 63 (65) 67 (68) 69cm
[24.75 (25.5) 26.5 (26.75) 27.25in]

Needles
Circular needle 4mm (US 6) [UK 8], 60cm [24in]
Circular needle 5mm (US 8) [UK 6], 80cm [32in]
If not using Magic Loop technique, use double-pointed needles in the same sizes for edgings.
Tapestry needle for finishing.

Knitting Gauge/Tension
14 sts x 18 rows on 5mm (US 8) [UK 6] needles in charted pattern = 10 × 10cm (4 × 4in)

Yarn
Rauma Garn's Vams

Colour A
(Main colour) 37 (Blue):
250 (300) 350 (350) 400g
Colour B
(Large diamonds) 01 (Natur)
150 (150) 200 (200) 250g
Colour C
(Small diamonds) 113 (Melon)
50 (50) 50 (50) 50g

Info
The slipover is worked from the bottom up.

Colour pattern knitting is also called Fair Isle. If you usually carry the yarn in your left hand, work with both colours over your left index finger always in the same order. The colour closest to you (and the needle) will dominate visually, the other, usually the lighter colour, will recede somewhat. There is no twisting involved and the yarn not in use will run straight across the purl side. Be careful not to pull either yarn tight when changing colours. If you carry the yarns in your right hand, always bring the dominant colour from beneath the other and the secondary colour *over* the dominant. If you are comfortable with both styles of knitting, you can pick the dominant (darker) color from your left index and carry the secondary color on your right index to accomplish the same effect.

The last st of every row is worked with both colors held together, so that all colour strands reach all the way to the edge to maintain an even tension. The first st of every row is worked with only one colour/strand, matching the charted pattern.

When binding off at the underarm, bind off with both colors held together.

Body
Cast on 144 (160) 176 (192) 208 sts on 4mm (US 6) [UK 8] needles, with Italian cast-on and Colour A. Join in a rnd and place a marker for beg of rnd.

Work 2 rnds double-knit:
Rnd 1. *K1, sl 1 p-wise with yarn in front of work. Rep from * to end of rnd.
Rnd 2. Sl 1 p-wise with yarn behind work, p1. Rep from * to end of rnd.

Work 8cm [3.25in] k1, p1 ribbing.
Change to 5mm (US 8) [UK 6] needles and start charted pattern, repeating it to end of rnd.

K even in pattern until work measures 33 (34) 35 (36) 37cm [13 (13.25) 13.75 (14.125) 14.5in] including ribbing.

Now bind off sts on both sides for the armhole, removing beg-of-rnd marker as you work. When binding off, bind off with both strands/colours held together.

K 68 (76) 84 (92) 100 sts (front), bind off 9 sts (underarm), k63 (71) 79 (87) 95 sts and place sts on a holder (back), bind off 9 sts (underarm).

The reason for the unequal number of sts is that, when you bind off the second time, you are binding off some of the sts on the front section that you knit at the beginning of the rnd.

Total 63 (71) 79 (87) 95 sts each
for the front and the back.
The sts on the needle are for the front.

Now work stockinette back and forth, continuing the charted pattern already established.

The first and the last sts of each row are selvage sts, worked as k sts in every row. The last st of every row is worked with the two strands held together, so that all colour strands carried on the back reach all the way to the edge and maintain an even tension. The first st on every row is worked with only one colour/strand, matching the charted pattern.

When binding off at the underarm, bind off with both strands held together.

Front Armholes and Shoulders
K2 rows stockinette.

Now bind off on both sides to shape the armholes:
Row 1 (rs). Bind off 1 st, k to end of row.
Row 2 (ws). Bind off 1 st, p to end of row.

Work Rows 1–2 a total 4 (5) 6 (7) 8 times.
Total 55 (61) 67 (73) 79 sts.

Now work even in stockinette and pattern until work measures 51 (53) 55 (56) 57cm [20 (21) 21.75 (22) 22.5in], including ribbing. End with a ws row.

Divide the front into left and right sections and bind off for the front neckline:

K22 (25) 28 (31) 34 sts and place these sts on a holder (right shoulder). Bind off 11 sts for the neck opening and k22 (25) 28 (31) 34 sts (left shoulder).

Left Shoulder
Row 1 (ws). P to end of row.
Row 2 (rs). Bind off 2 sts, k until 1 st remains in row, k1.
Row 3. P to end of row.
Row 4. Bind off 1 st, k to end of row.
Work Rows 3–4 a total 4 times.
Total 16 (19) 22 (25) 28 sts.
Work even now in stockinette and following chart until work measures 63 (65) 67 (68) 69cm [24.75 (25.5) 26.5 (26.75) 27in] above ribbing. Place sts on a holder.

Right Front Shoulder
Replace right shoulder sts on the needle. Start on the knit side.
Row 1 (rs). K to end of row.
Row 2. Bind off 2 sts, p to end of row.
Row 3. K1, k to end of row.
Row 4. Bind off 1 st, p to end of row.
Work Rows 3–4 a total 4 times.
Total 16 (19) 22 (25) 28 sts.

Now work even in pattern until work measures 63 (65) 67 (68) 69cm [24.75 (25.5) 26.5 (26.75) 27in] from ribbing. Place sts on a holder.

Back
Replace back sts on the needle and attach yarn at the beg of a k row. Continue in pattern.

Work 2 rows stockinette.

Now bind off on both edges to shape armholes:
Row 1 (rs). Bind off 1 st, k to end of row.
Row 2 (ws). Bind off 1 st, p to end of row.

Work rows 1–2 a total 4 (5) 6 (7) 8 times.
55 (61) 67 (73) 79 sts.

Work even in pattern until back measures 61 (63) 65 (66) 67cm [24 (24.75) 25.5 (26) 26.25in] from ribbing. End with a p row.

Now divide sts into right and left back shoulders and bind off for the neck opening as follows:
K16 (19) 22 (25) 28 sts and place them on a holder (right back shoulder).

Bind off 23 sts so that 16 (19) 22 (25) 28 sts remain on the needle, that is, 16 (19) 22 (25) 28 sts each for right and left back shoulders. Sts remaining on needle are for the left back shoulder.

Work left shoulder even until the back is as long as the front. Break yarn and place sts on a holder.

Replace right shoulder sts on needles and work even until as long as the front shoulder. Don't break yarn.

Back and front shoulders are knitted together: Turn work to purl side. Place sts for right front on a needle so that sts for the right front shoulder and sts for the right back shoulder are on separate needles, knit sides facing, but both in the left hand.

Take a new needle – a larger size if you have one, or the ribbing needle will work – and k the first 2 sts tog, one from each needle. K the next 2 sts tog, one from each needle, then bind off the first by passing the first over the newest st. Continue this until all the shoulder sts are bound off 2 by 2 tog. Rep on the right side.

Neck
On 4mm (US 6) [UK 8] needles, pick up and k76 (78) 80 (82) 84 sts around the neck opening. Pick up every st on the horizontal edges and every 2nd st on the vertical sides. Join in a rnd and place a marker. Work 18 rnds k1, p1 ribbing.

Turn the ribbing over to the wrong side, and k the neckband to the edge of the neck opening with 5mm (US 8) [UK 6] needles, much as you knit the shoulders tog:
Pick up the first st from the neckline picked-up sts from the p side and knit it tog with the first st on the left needle. Be careful to match the ribbing sts top and bottom.
*Pick up another st onto the left needle and k2tog with the 1st st on the left needle. Lift the first st over the new st on the right needle, so the first st is now bound off.
Rep from * until all collar sts are bound off.

Armholes
Pick up and k86 (90) 94 (98) 102 sts on 4mm (US 6) [UK 8] needles around the armhole. Skip every 3rd st. Join into a rnd and place a marker for beg of rnd.

Work 5 rnds of k1, p1 ribbing.

Work 2 rnds of double-knit as follows:
Rnd 1. *K1, sl 1 p-wise with yarn in front of work. Rep from * to end of rnd.
Rnd 2. *Sl 1 p-wise with yarn behind work, p1. Rep from * to end of rnd.

End with Italian bind-off.

Work ribbing for the other armhole the same way.

Finishing
Use tapestry needle to work in all loose tails on the purl side.

Chart

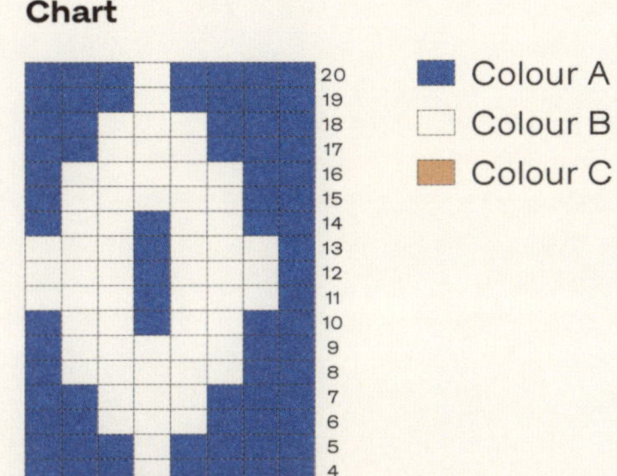

Hilda Sweater

Sizes
XS-S (M-L) XL-XXL

Measurements
Chest: 114 (125) 137cm
[41 (49.25) 53.5in]
Length: 58 (60) 62cm
[22.75 (23.6) 24.5in]

Needles
Circular needle 4mm (US 6) [UK 8], 60cm [24in]
Circular needle 6.5mm (US 10.5) [UK 3], 80cm [32in]
If not using Magic Loop technique, use double-pointed (dp) needles in the same sizes for shorter rnds.
Tapestry needle for finishing.

Knitting Gauge/Tension
14 sts x 18 rows on 6.5mm (US 10.5) [UK 3] needles in pattern = 10 × 10cm (4 × 4in)

Yarn
Rauma Garn's Vams
Colour A
(Main colour) 01 (Natur):
400 (450) 550g

Colour B
(large diamonds) 45 (Signal green):
200 (250) 350g

Colour C
(little diamonds) 77 (Midnight blue):
50 (50) 50g

Info
The vest is worked from the top down. The neckband is worked back and forth in stockinette and colour pattern. The sweater is then joined into a rnd and worked circularly. The rollover collar is worked last.

The first and the last sts of each row are selvage sts, worked as k sts in every row.

Colour pattern knitting is also called Fair Isle. If you usually carry the yarn in your left hand, work with both colours over your left index finger always in the same order. The colour closest to you (and the needle) will dominate visually, the other, usually the lighter colour, will recede somewhat. There is no twisting involved and the yarn not in use will run straight across the purl side. Be careful not to pull either yarn tight when changing colours. If you carry the yarns in your right hand, always bring the dominant colour from beneath the other and the secondary colour *over* the dominant. If you are comfortable with both styles of knitting, you can pick the dominant (darker) color from your left index and carry the secondary color on your right index to accomplish the same effect.

Raglan Shoulders
Cast on 59 (65) 65 sts with Colour A on 6.5mm (US 10.5) [UK 3] needles, and place markers:
Cast on 2 sts, place marker (left front).
Cast on 15 (17) 17 sts, place marker (left sleeve).
Cast on 25 (27) 27 sts, place marker (back).
Cast 15 (17) 17 (right sleeve).
Cast on 2 sts (right front).
Turn work and p1 row.

Now knit back and forth in stockinette and charted pattern for the next 13 rows, following charts on p. 87, and increasing at the same time. You've placed markers separating the charts. Work from bottom right of each.

When these charts are completed, join the ends: Don't turn the work after Row 13, stay on the knit side, break the yarn and move the left front and the left sleeve sts onto the right needle. This is now the beg of the rnd, Place a marker there that looks different from the others. Total 127 (133) 133 sts.

Re-attach yarn here and work following the established pattern, fitting new sts into the charted pattern as they increase in number.

K the back sts, the right sleeve and the right front sts, cast on 9 (11) 11 sts, join into a rnd with the left front sts and k to rnd marker. Total 136 (144) 144 sts.

Follow raglan incs and colour pattern shown on charts (overleaf):
Rnd 1. *K1, make 1 left, k to 1 st before marker, make 1 rt. Rep from * 3 more times.
Rnd 2. K to end of rnd.

Work these 2 rnds a total 16 (19) 21 times. Total 264 (296) 312 sts.

You've now increased for the raglan 23 (26) 28 times in all: 71 (79) 83 sts each for the front and back and 61 (69) 73 sts for each sleeve.

Body
Now separate the body and sleeve sts. Continue pattern and remove markers as you go:
K the back sts, place right arm sts on a holder, cast on 9 (9) 13 sts at underarm, k the front sts, place left sleeve sts on a holder, cast on 4 (4) 6 sts, place a new beg-of-rnd marker, cast on 5 (5) 7 sts and join into a rnd again. Total 160 (176) 192 sts for the body.

K even in pattern until work measures 49 (51) 53cm [19.25 (20) 21in] from the back of the neck opening.

Change to 4mm (US 6) [UK 8] needles and k 1 rnd increasing 12 (12) 14 sts evenly distributed by working make 1 rt.

A patterned sweater with a rolled collar

Total 172 (188) 206 sts.

Work 9cm [3.5in] in k1, p1 ribbing.

Work 2 rnds double-knit:
Rnd 1. *K1, sl 1 p-wise with yarn in front. Rep from * to end of rnd.
Rnd 2. *Sl 1 p-wise with yarn behind work, p1. Rep from* to end of rnd.
End with Italian bind-off.

Sleeves
Replace sts for one sleeve on 6.5mm (US 10.5) [UK 3] needles. From sts cast on at body underarm, pick up and k9 (9) 13 sts with Colour A. Pick up right to left, on the k side. Place a marker with 4 (4) 6 sts to right of marker and 5 (5) 7 sts to the left. Total 70 (78) 86 sts.

Now knit around in stockinette and established pattern. K the 2 sts on each side of the marker in Colour A in all rnds. Dec every 6th (5th) 4th rnd a total 10 (12) 14 times as follows: K2tog, k in pattern until 2 sts before marker, k2tog left. Use Colour A for the two dec sts. Total 50 (54) 58 sts.

K even in pattern until sleeve measures 37 (38) 39cm [14.5 (15) 15.25in] .

Change to 4mm (US 6) [UK 8] needles and K 1 rnd. Now work 9cm (3.5in) k1, p1 ribbing.

Work 2 rnds double-knit as on body and end with Italian bind-off. Make the other sleeve using these directions.

Neck
Pick up and knit about 80 (86) 86 sts around the neck opening with Colour A, on 4mm (US 6) [UK 8] needles s. Work 22cm [8.5in] k1, p1 ribbing.

Work double-knit as on body and sleeves and end with Italian bind-off.

Finishing
Sew in all loose ends.

Left front shoulder XS–S

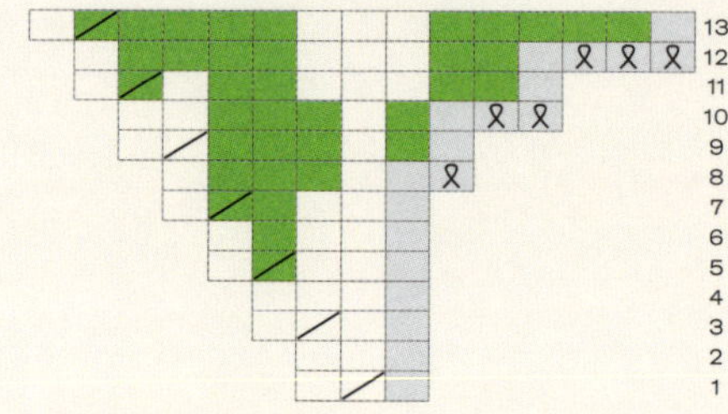

Right front shoulder XS–S

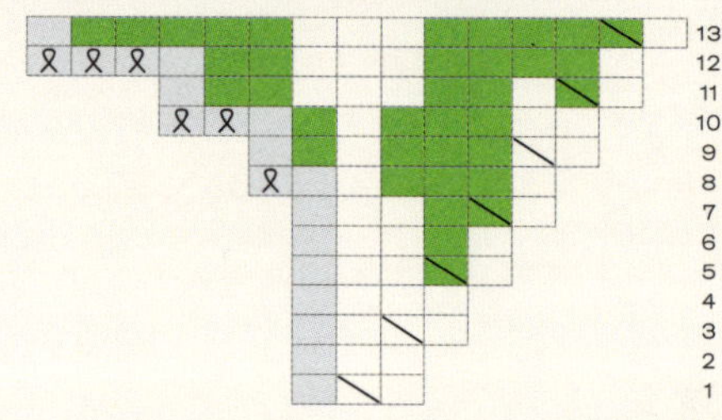

Left front shoulder (M–L) XL–XXL

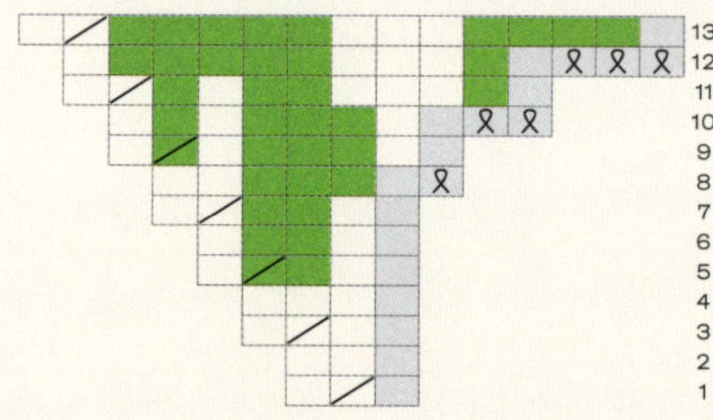

Right front shoulder (M–L) XL–XXL

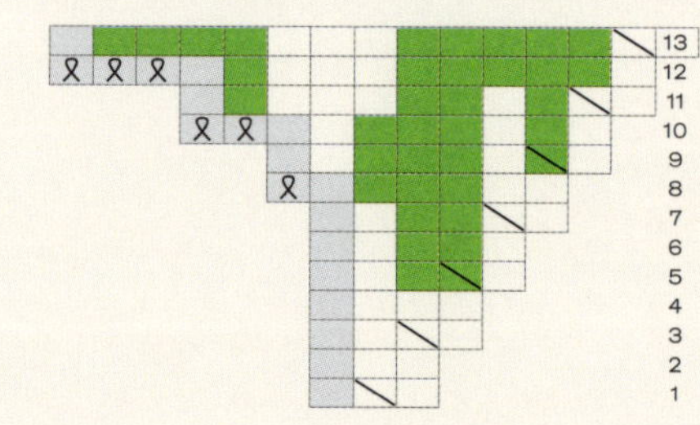

Raglan, right and left sleeve XS–S

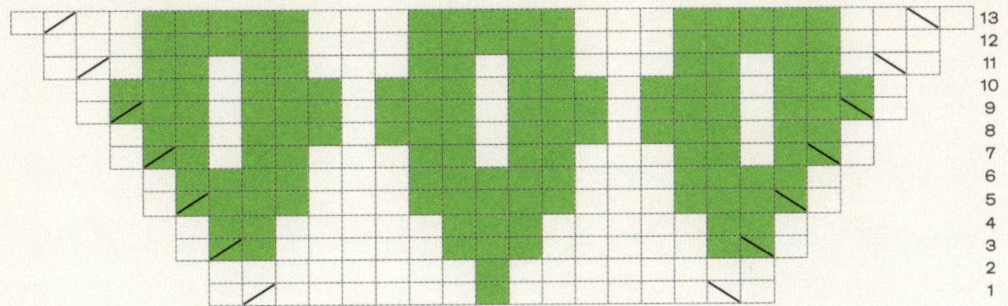

Pattern chart

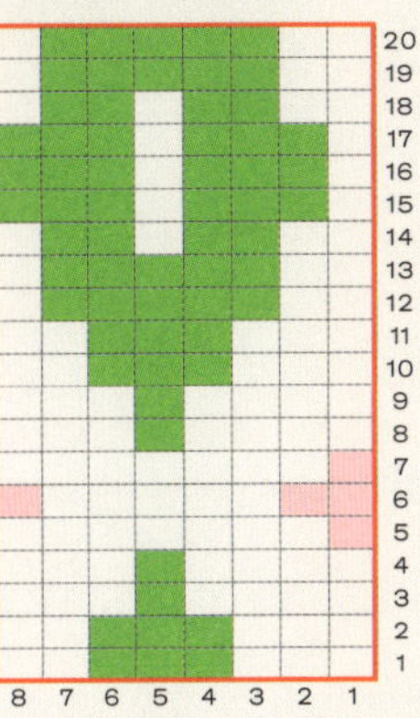

- Colour A
- Colour B
- Colour C
- inc right
- inc left
- repeat
- knit with both colours held together
- Cast on a new st with both colours held together.

Raglan right front (M–L) XL–XXL

Raglan back XS–S

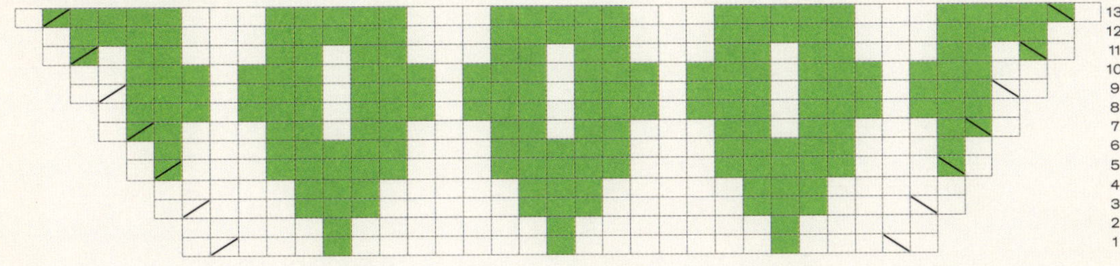

Raglan back (M–L) XL–XXL

A brushed sweater with a patterned circular yoke

Icelandic Hilda

Sizes
XS (S) M (L) XL (XXL)

Measurementss
Chest: 101 (109) 111 (117) 120 (127)cm
[39.75 (43) 43.75 (46) 47.25 (50)in]
Length: 54 (56) 58 (58) 60 (62)cm
[21.25 (22) 22.75 (23.5) 24.5in]

Needles
Circular needle 4mm (US 6) [UK 8], 60cm [24in]
Circular needle 5mm (US 8) [UK 6], 80cm [32in]
If not using Magic Loop technique, use double-pointed needles in the same sizes for neckline and sleeves.
Tapestry needle for finishing.

Knitting Gauge/Tension
14 sts x 18 rows on 5mm (US 8) [UK 6] needles in stockinette = 10 × 10cm (4 × 4 in)

Yarns
HipKnitShop's Fluff

Colour A (Main colour)
Red version (p. 34 and p. 63): Lipstick Red
Pink version (p. 96): Vanilla Flavour
300 (300) 350 (400) 450 (500)g
Colour B (Pattern colour)
Red version: Vanilla Flavour
Pink version: Jelly Bean Green
50 (50) 50 (50) 50 (50)g

Other Equipment: Mohair brush

Info
The sweater is worked circularly from the top down, with short rows to shape the neckline.

Colour pattern knitting is also called Fair Isle. If you usually carry the yarn in your left hand, work with both colours over your left index finger always in the same order. The colour closest to you (and the needle) will dominate visually, the other, usually the lighter colour, will recede somewhat. There is no twisting involved and the yarn not in use will run straight across the purl side. Be careful not to pull either yarn tight when changing colours. If you carry the yarns in your right hand, always bring the dominant colour from beneath the other and the secondary colour *over* the dominant. If you are comfortable with both styles of knitting, you can pick the dominant (darker) color from your left index and carry the secondary color on your right index to accomplish the same effect.

Neck
Cast on 60 (64) 64 (68) 68 (72) sts on 4mm (US 6) [UK 8] needles with Colour A. Place a marker at what will be the centre back and join in a rnd. Work 10cm [4in] in k1, p1 ribbing.

K 1 rnd joining the 2 edges of the ribbing: Fold the ribbing over toward the p side and k sts on the needle tog with matching sts in the cast-on rnd. Take care to match sts rib by rib.

Yoke
Change to 5mm (US 8) [UK 6] needles and k 1 rnd, increasing 4 sts spaced evenly around, by make 1 rt. Total 64 (68) 68 (72) 72 (76) sts.

Place a turn marker after 32 (34) 34 (36) 36 (38) sts.

Now make short rows for the back of the neckline. Use the German Short Rows method as follows:
K to 12 sts before turn marker, turn.
P to 12 sts before turn marker, turn.
K to 9 sts before turn marker, turn.
P to 9 sts before turn marker, turn.
K to 6 sts before turn marker, turn.
P to 6 sts before marker, turn.
K to beg of rnd.

Start charted pattern (from lower right and working upward on chart). Rep chart 16 (17) 17 (18) 18 (19) times to end of rnd. The slated boxes indicate incs by make 1 rt. within the pattern. Total 176 (187) 187 (198) 198 (209) sts.

When you've finished working the chart, continue increasing:

K3 (4) 4 (4) 5 (5) rnds even.
Next rnd. *Make 1 rt, k 11. Rep from * to end of rnd.
K5 (5) 6 (6) 6 (6) rnds.
Next rnd. *Make 1 rt, k12. Rep from * to end of rnd.
K7 (7) 8 (8) 8 (8) rnds even.

Sizes S, M and XXL only
Next rnd. K6, make 1 rt, k to end of rnd.

Sizes L and XL only
Next rnd. K to end of rnd.

All Sizes
Total 208 (222) 222 (234) 234 (248) sts.

Divide the sts into body and sleeves:
K30 (33) 33 (35) 35 (37) sts (rt half of back); place the next 44 (45) 45 (47) 47 (50) sts on a holder (rt sleeve); cast on 8 (8) 12 (12) 14 (14) sts for underarm; k60 (66) 66 (70) 70 (74) sts (front); place the next 44 (45) 45 (47) 47 (50) sts on a holder (left sleeve); cast on 8 (8) 12 (12) 14 (14) sts for underarm, k30 (33) 33 (35) 35 (37) sts (left side of the back).
Total 136 (148) 156 (164) 168 (176) sts for body.

Start of the rnd is still marked at centre back.

Body
K even down in stockinette, until work measures 47 (49) 51 (51) 53 (55)cm [18.5 (19.25) 20 (20) 21 (21.75)in] from the front neck edge including the ribbed neckband.

Change to 4mm (US 6) [UK 8] needles and work 10cm [4in] in k1, p1 ribbing. Bind off loosely in ribbing.

Sleeves
Replace sts for 1 sleeve back on 5mm (US 8) [UK 6] needles.

Pick up and k4 (4) 6 (6) 7 (7) sts starting at centre of the cast-on underarm sts on the body, k sleeves sts and pick up and k4 (4) 6 (6) 7 (7) sts from the remaining underarm cast-on sts. Place marker here and join into a rnd.
Total 52 (53) 57 (59) 61 (64) sts.

Now shape the sleeve: dec every 8th (8th) 8th (7th) 7th (5th) rnd 8 (8) 8 (9) 9 (10) times.

Dec rnd. K1, k2tog, k to 3 sts before marker, k2tog left, k1.
Total 36 (37) 41 (41) 43 (44) sts.

From this point, k even until sleeve measures 37 (38) 38 (38) 39 (39)cm [14.5 (15)15 (15) 15.5in].

Change to size 4mm (US 6) [UK 8] needles.

K 1 rnd, in sizes S–XL only , k2tog at beg of rnd to make a multiple of 2.

Work 10cm [4in] in k1, p1 ribbing. Bind off in ribbing.

Make the second sleeve in the same way.

Finishing
Sew all ends into purl side. Wash sweater according to yarn manufacturer's instructions. Lay flat to dry, then brush the fibres up with a mohair brush working from the neckband down. Take small sections at a time.

Chart

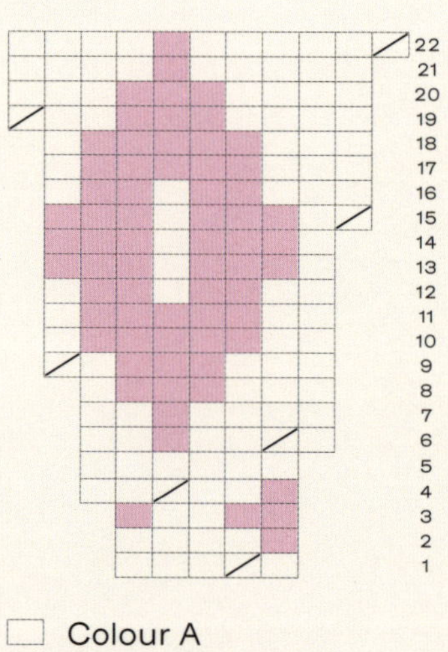

Colour A
Colour B
Make 1 right

A turtleneck sweater in brushed mohair

Mohairy Sweater

Sizes
XS (S) M (L) XL (XXL)

Measurements
Chest: 99 (109) 119 (126) 135 (141)cm
[39 (43) 47 (49.25) 53 (55.5)in]
Length: 52 (53) 54 (55) 56 (57)cm
[20.5 (21) 21.25 (21.75) 22 (22.5)in]
Sleeve **Length:** 52 (52) 52 (52) 53 (53)cm
[20.5 (20.5) 20.5 (20.5) 21 (21)in]

Needles
Circular needle size 3.5mm (US 4)
[UK 9 or 10], 60cm [24in]
Circular needle 4.5mm (US 7) [UK 7],
80cm [32in]
If not using Magic Loop technique,
use double-pointed needles in the
same sizes for shorter rounds.
Tapestry needle for finishing.

Knitting Gauge/Tension
17 sts x 20 rows on 4.5mm (US 7) [UK 7]
needles in stockinette = 10 × 10cm (4 × 4in)

Yarn
Honse x Spektakelstrik's Thick Mohair
400 (450) 500 (550) 550 (600)g

Other Equipment
Mohair brush

Info
This sweater is knitted from the top down.

Knit the first and last sts of every row.

Back
Cast on 30 (33) 33 (33) 36 (36) sts on
4.5mm (US 7) [UK 7] needles. P1 row.

Now inc on both sides on both sides on both
k and p sides to shape top of the shoulders.
Row 1 (rs). (Inc) K4, make 1 left, k until
4 sts remain in row, make 1 rt, k4.
Row 2 (ws). (Inc) K1, p3, p-make 1 rt, p
until 4 sts remain, p-make 1 left, p3, k1.

Work Rows 1–2 total 9 (10) 11 (12) 13
(14) times = 66 (73) 77 (81) 88 (92) sts.

Work even in stockinette (k on rs, p on
ws) until work measures 20 (21) 22
(23) 24 (25)cm [8 (8.25) 8.75 (9)
9.5 (9.75)in] to top of centre back.

Now inc on both sides for the armholes:
Row 1 (rs). K4, make 1 left, k until
4 sts remain, make 1 rt, k4.
Row 2 (ws). K1, p until 1 st remains, k1.

Work Rows 1–2 a total 5 (6) 7 (8) 9 (10)
times = 76 (85) 91 (97) 106 112) sts.

Break yarn and place back sts on a holder.

Left Front Shoulder
With 4.5mm (US 7) [UK 7] needles
pick up and k19 (21) 23 (25) 27 (29)
sts along the sloped shoulder sts
on the knit side of the left back.
Work even in stockinette until the left
front piece measures 6cm [2.5in].
End with a p row.

Now inc to form front neckline.
Row 1 (rs). K4, make 1 left, knit to end of row.
Row 2 (ws). K1, p until 1 st remains, k1.
Work Rows 1–2 a total 9 times = 28 (30) 32
(34) 36 (38) sts.

Break yarn and place sts on a holder.

Right Front Shoulder
With 4.5mm (US 7) [UK 7] needles
pick up and k19 (21) 23 (25) 27 (29)
sts along the sloped shoulder sts on
the knit side of the right back.
Work even in stockinette until the right
front piece measures 6cm [2.5in].
End with a p row.

Now inc to shape the front neckline:
Row 1 (rs). K until 4 sts remain, make 1 rt, k4.
Row 2 (ws). K1, p until 1 st remains, k1.
Work Rows 1–2 a total 9 times =
28 (30) 32 (34) 36 (38) sts.
Next row. K entire row, then cast on 10
(13) 13 (13) 16 (16) sts at the neckline end
of the row, replace the left front shoulder
sts on the needle and k to end of row.
Total 66 (73) 77 (81) 88 (92) sts.

The front pieces are now joined. Work even until front measures 20 (21) 22 (23) 24 (25)cm [8 (8.25) 8.75 (9) 9.5 (9.75)in] from the shoulder joint.

Now inc to shape the underrms as on the back section:
Row 1 (rs). K4, make 1 left, k until 4 sts remain, make 1 rt, k4.
Row 2 (ws). K1, p until 1 st remains, k1.

Work Rows 1–2 a total 5 (6) 7 (8) 9 (10) times = 76 (85) 91 (97) 106 (112) sts.

Body
Join front and back sections:
K front sts, cast on 8 (8) 10 (10) 12 (12) sts, place back sts on needle and across back, cast on 4 (4) 5 (5) 6 (6) sts, place beg-of-rnd marker, cast on 4 (4) 5 (5) 6 (6) sts and join into a rnd.
Total 168 (186) 202 (214) 236 (248) sts.

K even in stockinette until work measures 42 (43) 44 (45) 46 (47)cm [16.5 (17) 17.25 (17.75) 18 (18.5)in].

Change to 3.5mm (US 4) [UK 9 or 10] needles and k 1 rnd, increasing 12 (14) 16 (18) 20 (22) sts evenly distributed by make 1 left.
Total 180 (200) 218 (230) 254 (268) sts.

Work 10cm [4in] in k1, p1 ribbing.

Work 2 rnds double-knit:
Rnd 1. *K1, sl 1 p-wise with yarn in front. Rep from * to end of rnd.
Rnd 2. *Sl 1 p-wise with yarn in back, p1,. Rep from * to end of rnd.

End with Italian bind-off.

Sleeves
Starting at the middle of the underarm sts, pick up and k76 (80) 84 (88) 92 (96) sts along the arm hole on 4.5mm (US 7) [UK 7], needles. Skip every 3rd st.

Place a turn marker at the halfway mark, that is after 38 (40) 42 (44) 46 (48) sts, and a marker for the beg/end of rnd, (centre underarm sts).

Now work short rows to shape the sleeve cap. You can use the German Short Rows method as follows:
K to 6 sts beyond the turn marker, turn.
P to 6 sts beyond the turn marker, turn.
K to 9 sts beyond the turn marker, turn.
P to 9 sts beyond the turn marker, turn.
K to 12 sts beyond the turn marker, turn.
P to 12 sts beyond the turn marker, turn.

Continue in this way, turning 3 sts after the previous turn each time until there are 7 (8) 8 (8) 9 (9) turns on each side of the marker. K to end of rnd. Remove the turn marker, so only the rnd marker remains.

Now dec every 7th (6th) 6th (5th) 5th (4th) rnd a total 12 (14) 15 (17) 18 (20) times to shape the sleeve: K1, k2tog, k to 3 sts before marker, k2tog left, k1.
Total 52 (52) 54 (54) 56 (56) sts.

Continue even around until the sleeve measures 42 (42) 42 (42) 43 (43) cm [16.5 (16.5) 16.5 (16.5) 17 (17) in], measured along the underarm.

Change to 3.5mm (US 4) [UK 9 or 10] needles.
Work 10cm [4in] in k1, p1 ribbing.

Work 2 rnds double-knit as on lower edge of body ribbing.
End with Italian bind-off. Knit the second sleeve following the same directions.

Neck
Pick up and k98 (102) 102 (102) 110 (110) sts along the neck opening from the k side on 3.5mm (US 4) [UK 9 or 10] needles needles.
Work 6.5 (6.5) 6.5 (6.5) 7 (7)cm [2.5 (2.5) 2.5 (2.5) 2.75 (2.75)in] in k1, p1 ribbing.
Work 2 rnds double-knit as on lower edge of body ribbing.
End with Italian bind-off.

Finishing
With tapestry needle, sew all ends into reverse side of knit. Wash the sweater following yarn manufacturer's instructions, lay the sweater to dry, then brush the fibres up with the mohair brush, working from top down. Take small sections at a time.

Icelandic Hilda→ 88

A light, cropped sweater

Crew Sweater

Sizes
XS (S) M (L) XL (XXL)

Measurements
Chest: 99 (104) 111 (115) 122 (127)cm [39 (41) 43.75 (45.25) 48 (50)in]
Length: 42 (44) 45 (47) 48 (50)cm [16.5 (17.25) 17.75 (18.5) 19 (19.75)in]
Sleeve length: 46 (46) 47 (48) 48 (49)cm [18 (18) 18.5 (19) 19 (19.25)in]

Needles
Circular needle size 3.5mm (US 4) [UK 9 or 10], 60cm [24in]
Circular needle 5mm (US 8) [UK 6], 60cm [24in]
If not using Magic Loop technique, use double-pointed (dp) needles in the same sizes for neckline and sleeves.
Tapestry needle for finishing.

Knitting Gauge/Tension
17 sts x 23 rows on 5mm (US 8) [UK 6] needles with 2 strands held together in stockinette = 10 × 10cm (4 × 4in)

Yarns
Biches & Bûches' Le Gros Silk & Mohair, Colour: Light Pink
300 (350) 350 (400) 450 (500)g

held together with

Biches & Bûches' Le Petit Silk & Mohair, Colour: Very Light Pink
100 (125) 125 (150) 150 (175)g

Info
The sweater is knitted from the top down with the 2 yarns held together. The back is worked first, with the front picked up from the back shoulders. After the underarm, the body is worked circularly. Stitches are later picked up for the sleeves and neckband.

The first and the last sts of each row are selvage sts, worked as k sts in every row.

Back Shoulders
Cast on 70 (72) 74 (76) 78 (80) sts on 5mm (US 8) [UK 6] needles.
Work even in stockinette (k on rs, p on ws), until the back is about 7 (17.5) 18 (18.5) 19 (19.5)cm [6.75 (7) 7.25 (7.5) 7.75 (8)in] long. End with a p row on ws.

Now inc to shape the armhole:
Row 1 (rs). K3, make 1 left, k until 3 sts remain, make 1 rt, k3.
Row 2. K1, p until 1 st remains, k1.
Work Rows 1–2 a total 5 (6) 7 (8) 9 (10) times = 80 (84) 88 (92) 96 (100) sts.
Break yarn and place sts on a holder.

Left Front Shoulder
Count 21 (22) 23 (24) 25 (26) sts in from the left edge of the cast-on edge of the back. The knit side of the back piece should be facing you as you count.

With 5mm (US 8) [UK 6] needles, pick up and k the 21 (22) 23 (24) 25 (26) sts you counted, working from the centre back toward the left edge.

Starting with a p row on the ws, work 10 (11) 11 (11) 11 (12)cm [4 (4.25) 4.25 (4.25) 4.25 (4.75)in] in stockinette. End with a p row.

Now make incs at beg of the k side rows, to form the neck opening.
Row 1 (rs). (Inc) K3, make 1 left, k to end of row.
Row 2 (ws). K1, p until 1 st remains, k1.
Work Rows 1–2 total 9 times = 30 (31) 32 (33) 34 (35) sts.

Break yarns and place sts on a holder.

Right Front Shoulder
On the k side (rs), pick up and k21 (22) 23 (24) 25 (26) sts from the right side of the back, starting at the outer edge and working toward the middle. The knit side of the back should be facing you.
Work 10 (11) 11 (11) 11 (12)cm [4 (4.25) 4.25 (4.25) 4.25 (4.75)in] in stockinette, starting with a p row on the wrong side. End with a p row.

Now inc at the end of the k side rows to shape the neckline:
Row 1 (rs). K until 3 sts remain in the row make 1 rt, k3.
Row 2 (ws). K1, p until 1 st remains in row, k1.
Work Rows 1–2 a total 9 times = 30 (31) 32 (33) 34 (35) sts.

Join the 2 front pieces:
On the right side, k until 2 sts remain, k2tog left, cast on 12 sts for front of neck opening – don't break the yarn – replace the left front shoulder sts on the left needle, k the first 2 sts tog and k to end of row.
Total 70 (72) 74 (76) 78 (80) sts.

Work even in stockinette until front measures 19 (19.5) 20 (20.5) 21 (21.5)cm [7.5 (7.75) 8 (8) 8.25 (8.5)in] from the shoulder seam. End with a p row on ws.

Now, inc, following the inc directions for shaping the armhole of the back.
Total 80 (84) 88 (92) 96 (100) sts.

Join the back and front sections:
Next row. K2tog, k until 2 sts remain, k2tog left, cast on 3 (3) 3 (4) 4 (4) sts for underarm, place marker for side 'seam', cast on 3 (3) 3 (4) 4 (4) more sts, replace the sts for the back onto the needle, k the first 2 sts tog, then k until 2 sts remain of the back sts, k2tog left, cast on 3 (3) 3 (4) 4 (4) sts, place marker (beg of rnd and side 'seam,' cast on 3 (3) 3 (4) 4 (4) sts more.
Total 168 (176) 184 (196) 204 (212) sts.

Body
Work around in stockinette (all k sts on rs) and dec at the 2 sides every 8th (9th) 9th (10th) 10th (11th) rnd 5 times:
K1, k2tog, k to 3 sts before marker, k2tog left, k2, k2tog, k until 3 sts before marker, k2tog left, k2, k2tog, knit to 3 sts before beg-of-rnd marker, k2tog left, k1.

The body portion should be 18 (20) 20 (22) 22 (24)cm [7 (8) 8 (8.75) 8.75 (9.5)in] long. If you want a longer sweater, a good way to do that is to allow a couple more rnds between dec rnds.

Change to 3.5mm (US 4) [UK 9 or 10] needles and work 6cm [2.5in] in k1, p1 ribbing.

Work 2 rnds double-knit:

Rnd 1. *K1, sl 1 p-wise with yarn in front. Rep from * end of rnd.
Rnd 1. * sl 1 p-wise with yarn behind work, p1. Rep from * to end of rnd.
End with Italian bind-off.

Sleeves
Start at the centre of the underarm (at the marker). Pick up and k3 (3) 3 (4) 4 (4) sts from the k side on 5mm (US 8) [UK 6] needles (working from right to left), then pick up and k7 (8) 9 (10) 11 (11) sts along the slanted edge with the incs, then pick up and k40 (42) 44 (44) 46 (47) sts along the armhole and over the shoulder, until you reach the inc rows on the other side. Place a turn marker in the centre of these, at the top of the armhole. (Be careful not to place it at the shoulder seam, as the front and the back sections are not the same length), pick up and k7 (8) 9 (10) 11 (11) sts along the 2nd slanted section with incs and finally pick up and knit 3 (3) 3 (4) 4 (4) sts on the last half of the sts cast on at the underarm. Place a marker for beg of rnd.
Total 60 (64) 68 (72) 76 (80) sts.

Now work short rows to shape the sleeve cap. The German short rows method is recommended:
K to turn marker, k4, turn.
P to turn marker, k4, turn.
K to turn marker, k8, turn.
P to turn marker, k8, turn.

Continue this way, turning 4 sts beyond the preceding turn until you have turned a total 5 (6) 6 (6) 6 (7) times on each side.

After the last turn, k circularly again to end of rnd. Remove turn marker.

K down in stockinette while decreasing every 18th (16th) 14th (13th) 12th (11th) rnd a total 5 (6) 7 (8) 8 (9) times: K1, k2tog, k until 3 sts remain in the rnd, k2tog left, k1 = 50 (52) 54 (56) 60 (62) sts.

K even until the inseam of the sleeve measures 42 (42) 43 (44) 44 (45)cm [16.5 (16.5) 17 (17) 17.25 (17.75)in].
Work 1 rnd and use k2tog to dec 10 (10) 12 (12) 14 (14) sts evenly spaced around.

Change to 3.5mm (US 4) [UK 9 or 10] needles.
Work 4cm [1.5in] in k1, p1 ribbing.

Now work 2 rnds double-knit as on bottom of body portion. End with Italian bind-off.

Work the second sleeve the same way.

Neck
On 3.5mm (US 4) [UK 9 or 10] needles, pick up and k96 (98) 100 (100) 102 (104) sts along the neckline edges, starting at a shoulder seam. Pick up every st on the horizontal portions, and every other st on the diagonals. Join into a rnd and place a marker

Work 21 rnds in k1, p1 ribbing.

Turn neckband to inside and knit it down with 5mm (US 8) [UK 6] needles as follows:

Pick up the first picked-up st on the p side of the neckline on the left needle and knit it tog with with the 1st ribbing st on the left needle. *Pick up the next neckline st with the left needle, k it tog with the next ribbing st on left needle. Pass the 1st st on the right needle over the new st, binding it off. Rep from * until all sts are bound off and the crew neck is completely hemmed.

Finishing
Work in all loose ends on the p side.

A pencil-skirt with an elastic waistband and a slit back

Crew Skirt

Sizes
XS (S) M (L) XL (XXL)

Measurements
Waist: 63-67 (67-72) 72-77 (77-83) 83-89 (89-93)cm [24.75-26.5 (26.5-28.25) 28.25-30.25 (30.25-32.5) 32.5-35 (35-36.25)in]
Length: 62 (64) 64 (64) 66 (68)cm [24.5 (25.25) 25.25 (25.25) 26 (26.75)in]

Needles
Circular needle size 3.5mm (US 4) [UK 9 or 10], 60cm [24in]
Circular needle 5mm (US 8) [UK 6], 60cm [24in]
Tapestry needle for finishing.

Knitting Gauge/Tension
17 sts x 23 rows on 5mm (US 8) [UK 6] needles with 2 strands held together in stockinette = 10 × 10cm (4 × 4in)

Yarns
Biches & Bûches' Le Gros Silk & Mohair, Colour Light pink:
200 (250) 250 (300) 350 (400)g

held together with

Biches & Bûches' Le Petit Silk & Mohair Colour Very light pink:
75 (100) 100 (125) 125 (150)g

Other Equipment
4cm [1.5in] wide elastic, 63 (68) 73 (79) 85 (91)cm [24.75 (26.75) 28.75 (31) 33.5 (36)in] long
sewing needle and thread for elastic

Info
The skirt is knitted from the top down with 2 yarns held together throughout.

A selvage or edge stitch is worked by slipping the first st of a row purlwise with the yarn in front of the needle. In the next row, from the purl side, the same st is knitted.

Waistband
Cast on 104 (112) 120 (128) 136 (144) sts on 5mm (US 8) [UK 6] circular needles. Join into a rnd and place a marker (beg/end of rnd marker), which will be at centre back of skirt).

K in stockinette (k every rnd) for 4cm [1.5in] P1 rnd (turnover rnd), then k in stockinette for another 4.5cm [1.75in].

Sew elastic together, overlapping the ends by 0.5cm [0.25in]. The elastic should be 2cm [0.75in] shorter than your waist measurement or 63 (68) 73 (79) 85 (91)cm [24.75 (26.75) 28.75 (31) 33.5 (36)in] long. Fold what you have knitted (the waistband) over around the elastic, creating a channel with the k side outside. Now k the 1st st on your needles with the first st from the cast-on edge (Pick up the st from the cast-on edge on the left needle and knit it tog with the first live st on the left needle.) Rep until all sts are knitted together and the entire channel is enclosed around the elastic. (Don't bind off)

Skirt
Now work short rows to make the back of the skirt fuller than the front. Use the German Short Rows technique:
K6 sts, turn.
P to marker, p6 more sts, turn.
K to marker, k12 more sts, turn.
P to marker, p12 more sts, turn.

Continue in this way, each time adding 6 more sts beyond the previous short row before turning until you have turned 4 (4) 4 (5) 5 (5) times on each side of the marker.
K to end of rnd.

Now place 2 new markers one on each side: K26 (28) 30 (32) 34 (36) sts, place marker, k52 (56) 60 (64) 68 (72) sts, place marker and k to end of rnd.

Now inc on both sides:
Rnds 1–5. K to end
Rnd 6. K to 1 st before side marker, make 1 rt, k2, make 1 left, k to 1 st before 2nd side marker, make 1 rt, k2, make 1 left, k to end of rnd.
Work Rnds 1–6 a total 7 (7) 8 (8) 8 (9) times = 132 (140) 152 (160) 168 (180) sts.

Work even in stockinette until skirt is 56 (56) 58 (58) 59 (59)cm [22 (22) 22.75 (22.75) 23.75 (23.75)in] from front centre waistband. Remove side markers.

Back Slit
Now make a slit in the centre of the back: K4, turn work to purl side. Work back and forth in rows:
Row 1 (ws). Sl 1 p-wise, k1, p1, k1, p1, k1, p1, k1, p to end of row. Cast on 8 sts, extending the row.
Row 2. Sl 1 p-wise, p1, k1, p1, k1, p1, k1, p1. K until 8 sts remain in row, work 8 sts in p1, k1 ribbing, matching the previous row.
Row 3. Sl 1 p-wise, k1, p1, k1, p1, k1, p1, k1, p until 8 sts remain, work 7 sts in k1, p1 ribbing, k1.
Work Rows 2–3 a total 8 (9) 9 (9) 9 (10) times.

Change to 3.5mm (US 4) [UK 9 or 10] needles. Work 8cm [3.25in] in k1, p1 ribbing, with the 1st edge st as sl 1 p-wise.
Dec 1 st somewhere in the first row to make multiple of 2 (for ribbing).

Work 2 rows double-knit:
Row 1. *K1, sl 1 p-wise with yarn in front of work. Rep from * to end of row.
Row 2. *Sl 1 p-wise with yarn behind work, p1. Rep from * to end of row.
End with Italian bind-off.

Finishing
Sew the top of the slit together. Sew all ends into the reverse side of work.

A basic sweater with an oversize boxy fit

Oversize Crew Sweater

Sizes
XS (S) M (L) XL (XXL)

Measurements
Chest: 106 (111) 115 (122) 127 (132)cm
[41.75 (43.75) 45.25 (48) 50 (52)in]
Length: 58 (59) 60 (61) 62 (63)cm
[22.75 (23.25) 23.625 (24) 24.5 (24.75)in]
Sleeve Length: 49 (49) 50 (51) 51 (52)cm
[19.25 (19.25) 19.75 (20) 20 (20) 20.5in]

Needles
Circular needle size 3.5mm (US 4)
[UK 9 or 10], 60cm [24in]
Circular needle 5mm (US 8) [UK 6],
60cm [24in]
If not using Magic Loop technique,
use double-pointed needles in the
same sizes for shorter rnds.
Tapestry needle for finishing.

Knitting Gauge/Tension
17 × 23 rows on 5mm (US 8) [UK 6]
needles with two yarns held together in
stockinette = 10 × 10cm (4 × 4 in)

Yarns
Biches & Bûches' Le Gros Silk & Mohair
Colour Dark Beige:
350 (400) 400 (450) 500 (550)g

held together with

Filcolana's Tilia
Colour 364 (Chai):
125 (150) 150 (175) 175 (200)g

Info
The sweater is worked from the top down with the two yarns held together. The back is knitted first, and the front is picked up and knitted down from the back shoulders. Sts are then picked up for the neckband and sleeves.

The first and the last sts of each row are selvage sts, worked as k sts in every row.

Back Shoulders
Cast on 76 (78) 80 (82) 84 (86) sts on 5mm (US 8) [UK 6] needles. Starting with a purl row, work even in stockinette (k on right side, p on wrong side) until piece measures 18 (18.5) 19 (19.5) 20 (20.5)cm [7 (7.25) 7.5 (7.75) 8 (8)in]. End with a p row.

Now inc to shape the armhole:
Row 1. (Inc) K3, make 1 left, k until 3 sts remain, make 1 rt, k3.
Row 2. k1, p until 1 st remains, k1.
Work Rows 1–2 a total 5 (6) 7 (8) 9 (10) times = 86 (90) 94 (98) 102 (106) sts.

Break yarn and place sts on a holder.

Left Front Shoulder
Count 24 (25) 26 (27) 28 (29) sts from the left edge of the back cast-on edge toward the middle, with the k side facing you.

With 5mm (US 8) [UK 6] needles pick up and k24 (25) 26 (27) 28 (29) sts from these sts, working from the neck side toward the armhole edge.
Starting with a p row, work stockinette even for 10 (11) 11 (11) 11 (12)cm [4 (4.25) 4.25 (4.25) 4.25 (4.75)in]. End with a p row.

Now inc at the beg of knit side rows to shape the neckline as follows:
Row 1 (rs). (Inc) K3, make 1 left, k to end of row.
Row 2 (ws). K1, p until 1 st remains, k1.

Work Rows 1–2 a total 9 times.
Break yarn and place sts on a holder.
33 (34) 35 (36) 37 (38) sts.

Right Front Shoulder
From the knit side and the right side of the back, with 5mm (US 8) [UK 6] needles pick up and k24 (25) 26 (27) 28 (29) sts. Start at the outer edge and work toward the middle. The knit side of the back should face you.

Starting with a p row, work stockinette even for 10 (11) 11 (11) 11 (12)cm [4 (4.25) 4.25 (4.25) 4.25 (4.75)in]. End with a p row.

Now make incs in the end of the knit side rows to shape the neckline as follows:
Row 1 (rs). K until 3 sts remain in row, make 1 right, k3.
Row 2 (ws). K1, p until 1 st remains, k1.
Work Rows 1–2 a total 9 times = 33 (34) 35 (36) 37 (38) sts.

Now join the front shoulder pieces:
On the right shoulder piece, k until 2 sts remain, k2tog left, cast on 12 sts, don't break the yarn, place the left front shoulder sts back on the needle, rs toward you, k the first 2 sts tog, and k to end of row.
Total 76 (78) 80 (82) 84 (86) sts.

Work even in stockinette until work measures 20 (20.5) 21 (21.5) 22 (22.5) cm [7.75 (8) 8.25 (8.5) 8.75 (9)in] from the shoulder seam. End with a p row. Now inc for underarm as you did on the back.
Total 86 (90) 94 (98) 102 (106) sts.

Join the back and front sections:
Next row. K2tog, k until 2 sts remain in row, k2tog left, cast on 6 (6) 6 (8) 8 (8) sts, place back shoulder sts on the needle, k the first 2 sts tog, and k until 2 sts of the back section remain, k2tog left, cast on 3 (3) 3 (4) 4 (4) sts (underarm), place marker for beg of rnd, cast on 3 (3) 3 (4) 4 (4) more sts.
Total 180 (188) 196 (208) 126 (224) sts.

Body
Work around in stockinette (k all rnds) until the sweater, measured from the back of the neck is 50 (51) 52 (53) 54 (55) 56 (57)cm [19.75 (20) 20.5 (21) 21.25 (21.75) 22 (22.5)in] long.

Change to 3.5mm (US 4) [UK 9 or 10] needles.

Work 1 rnd k1, p1 ribbing while increasing:
*K1, p1, k1, make 1 rt (as if on k side), k1, p1, k1, p1, k1, make 1 rt. Rep from * as many times as you can fit within the rnd, then work k1, p1 ribbing to end of rnd. If the last st in the rnd is a k st, make 1 rt once more.

Now work k1, p1 ribbing for total 8cm [3.25in].

Work 2 rnds double-knit as follows:
Rnd 1. *K1, sl 1 p-wise with yarn in front of work. Rep from * to end of rnd.
Rnd 2. *Sl 1 p-wise with yarn behind work, p1. Rep from * to end of rnd.
End with Italian bind-off.

Sleeves
Start at the middle of the underarm and pick up and k3 (3) 3 (4) 4 (4) sts on 5mm (US 8) [UK 6] needles, working from right to left on the knit side.

Pick up and k7 (8) 9 (10) 11 (12) sts along the slanted part with incs on the body, pick up and k22 (23) 24 (25) 26 (26) sts along the armhole to the top of the shoulder and place a marker (turn marker). (Avoid placing the marker at the shoulder seam as the front is longer than the back and extends part way across the shoulder.) Pick up and k22 (23) 24 (25) 26 (26) down to the remaining inc section. Pick up and k7 (8) 9 (10) 11 (12) sts along this slanted section with incs, and finally, pick up and k3 (3) 3 (4) 4 (4) sts from the last half of the sts cast on for the underarm and place a marker for beg/end of rnd.
Total 64 (68) 72 (78) 82 (84) sts.

Now work short rows back and forth to form the sleeve cap at the top. I recommend using the German Short Rows method, as follows:
K to turn marker, k4 sts, turn.
P to turn marker, k4 sts, turn.
K to turn marker, k8, turn.
P to turn marker, p8, turn.

Continue in this mode always turning 4 sts beyond the previous turn, until you have turned a total of 5 (6) 6 (6) 6 (7) times on each side. After the last turn, k to end of rnd and remove the turn marker.

K in stockinette while making decs every 11th (11th) 10th (9th) 9th (8th) row 9 (9) 11 (12) 12 (13) times as follows:
K1, k2tog, k until 3 sts remain in rnd, k2tog left, k1.
Total 46 (50) 50 (54) 58 (58) sts.

K even until the inner side of the sleeve measures 45 (45) 46 (47) 47 (48)cm [17.75 (17.75) 18 (18.5) 18.5 (19)in].

Change to 3.5mm (US 4) [UK 9 or 10] needles.Work 4cm [1.5in] in k1, p1 ribbing. Now work 2 rnds double-knit as on the bottom of the body section and end with Italian bind-off.

Work the second sleeve the same way.

Neck
Pick up and k98 (100) 100 (100) 100 (104) sts on 3.5mm (US 4) [UK 9 or 10] needles around the neckline. Pick up all sts on the horizontal and vertical sections and skip about every 3rd st on the slanted sections. Join into a rnd and place marker.

Work 21 rnds k1, p1 ribbing.

K the crew neck down and bind off at the same time on 5mm (US 8) [UK 6] needles: Working on the p side, pick up 1 st from the picked-up sts at the base of the crew neck onto the left needle, taking care to match first sts, etc, vertically. K this st tog with the first live st on the left needle. *Pick up one more st from the neck edge onto the left needle and k it tog with the new 1st live st on the left needle. Pass the first st over the new st on the right needle so that first st is bound off. Rep from * until all neck band sts are bound off.

Finishing
Sew in all loose ends on the purl side.

Bibi Scarf → 60

Bibi Sweater → 48

High-waisted pants with a loose fit

Crew Pants

Sizes
XS (S) M (L) XL (XXL)

Measurements
Waist: 63-67 (67-72) 72-77 (77-83) 83-89 (89-93)cm [24.75-26.25 (26.25-30.25) 30.25-32.75 (32.75-35) 35-36.5)in]
Inseam of leg: 80 (80) 81 (81) 82 (82)cm [31.5 (31.5) 32 (32) 32.25 (32.25)in]

Needles
Circular needle 4mm (US 6) [UK 8], 60cm [24in]
Circular needle 5mm (US 8) [UK 6], 60cm [24in]
Circular needles 3.5mm (US 4) [UK 9 or 10]. If not using Magic Loop technique, use double-pointed needles in the same sizes for short rnds.
Tapestry needle for finishing.

Other Equipment
4cm [1.5in] wide elastic, 63 (68) 73 (79) 85 (91)cm [24.75 (26.75) 28.75 (31) 33.5 (36) in] long sewing needle and thread for elastic

Knitting Gauge/Tension
18 sts x 25 rows on 5mm (US 8) [UK 6] in stockinette with both yarns held together = 10 × 10cm (4 × 4in)
If you cannot get exact tension, 19 sts to 10cm (4in) is better than 17 sts to 10cm (4in)

Yarns
Biches & Bûches' Le Gros Silk & Mohair Colour Dark Beige:
400 (450) 450 (500) 550 (600)g

held together with

Ficolana's Tilia, Colour 364 (Chai):
150 (175) 175 (200) 200 (225)g

Info
Crew Pants are worked from the top down. The pants can be made with ribbing at the cuffs to match the Crew Sweater or the Oversize Crew Sweater, or they can be worked with a hem for a cleaner look.

Waistband
Cast on 104 (112) 120 (128) 136 (144) sts on 4mm (US 6) [UK 8] needles, holding both yarns together, join into a rnd, and place a marker (beg/end of rnd marker to be at centre back).
K in stockinette (k every rnd) for 4cm [1.5in]
P1 rnd.

Change to 5mm (US 8) [UK 6] needles.
K in stockinette for another 4.5cm [1.75in].

Sew elastic together, overlapping the ends by 0.5cm [0.25in]. The elastic should be 2cm [0.75in] shorter than your waist measurement or 63 (68) 73 (79) 85 (91)cm [24.75 (26.75) 28.75 (31) 33.5 (36)in] long.

Fold what you have knitted (the waistband) over around the elastic, creating a channel with the k side outside. Now k the 1st st on your needles with the first st from the cast-on edge (Pick up the st from the cast-on edge on the left needle and k it tog with the first live st on the left needle.) Rep until all sts are knitted together and the entire channel is enclosed around the elastic.

Pants
Now work incs and short rows to make the pants roomier in back. Use the German Short Rows method as follows:
K8, turn.
P to rnd marker, p8, turn.
K to marker, k1, make 1 left, k14, turn.
P to marker, p1, p make 1 rt, p14, turn.
K to marker, k22, turn.
P to marker, p22, turn.
K to marker, k1, make 1 left, k28, turn.
P to marker, p1, p-make 1 rt, p28, turn.
K to marker, k37, turn.
P to marker, p37, turn.
K to marker, k1, make 1 left, k43, turn.
P to marker, p1, p-make 1 rt, p43, turn.
K to marker.
Total 110 (118) 126 (134) 142 (150) sts.

Now inc every 4th rnd in back and in front and every 12th rnd at the sides. In the first rnd, place 3 more markers, so the sts are divided in 4 sections:

From beg of rnd, k28 (30) 32 (34) 36 (38) sts, place side marker, k27 (29) 31 (33) 35 (37) sts and place centre-front marker, k27 (29) 31 (33) 35 (37) sts and place side marker.

Rnds 1–3. K to end of rnd.
Rnd 4. (Inc in front, , in back, and on the sides) K1, make 1 left, *k to 1 st before marker, make 1 rt, k2, make 1 left. Rep from * 2 more times, k to 1 st before rnd marker, make 1 rt, k1.
Rnds 5–7. K to end of rnd.
Rnd 8. (Inc in front and back):
K1, make 1 left, k to (side) marker, sl marker, k to 1 st before (front) marker, make 1 rt, k2, make 1 left, k to (side) marker, sl marker, k to 1 st before (beg of rnd) marker, make 1 rt, k1.
Rnds 9–11. K to end of rnd.
Rnd 12. (Inc in front and back) K1, make 1 left, k to (side) marker, sl marker, k to 1 st before (front) marker, make 1 rt, k2, make 1 left, k to (side) marker, sl marker, k to 1 st before rnd marker, make 1 rt, k1.

Work Rnds 1–12 a total 4 times.
Work Rnds 1–4 again.
Total 182 (190) 198 (206) 214 (222) sts.

Sizes XL (XXL) only: Work Rnds 5–8 once more.

All Sizes
182 (190) 198 (206) 218 (226) sts.

Now divide the work in 2 sections and work each leg separately as follows:
K to centre front marker, and set these sts on a holder (right leg). K to end of rnd (left leg).
Total 91 (95) 99 (103) 109 (113) sts for each leg.

Left Leg
Cast on 9 (11) 13 (13) 15 (17) sts at end of sts and place a marker in the middle of these new sts.
Total 100 (106) 112 (116) 124 (130) sts.

Pants with Ribbed Leg Edging
K even around in stockinette until the leg measures 70 (70) 71 (71) 72 (72)cm [27.5 (27.5) 28 (28) 28.25 (28.25)in] or 7cm [2.75in] shorter than your desired length.

Be aware that the pants will stretch 2.5-5cm [1–2in] in length after they are washed.

Change to 4mm (US 6) [UK 8] needles. Work 1 rnd in k1, p1 ribbing while increasing as follows: *K1, p1, k1, make 1 rt. Rep from * as many times as possible as you can fit into the rnd and work ribbing to end of rnd. If the last st is a knit st, make 1 rt once more (for k1, p1 ribbing, total sts must be multiple of 2.) Work 7cm [2.75in] continuing k1, p1 ribbing.

Work 2 rnds double-knit as follows:
Rnd 1. *K1, sl 1 p-wise with yarn in front of work. Rep from * to end of rnd.
Rnd 2. *Sl 1 p-wise with yarn behind work, p1. Rep from * to end of rnd.

End with Italian bind-off.

Legs Hemmed at Bottom
Work even in stockinette until pant leg is 77 (77) 78 (78) 79 (79)cm [30.25 (30.25) 30.75 (30.75) 31 (31)in] or desired length. Be aware that the pants will stretch 2.5-5cm [1-2in] in length after they are washed.

P1 rnd (hem edge).
Change to 4mm (US 6) [UK 8] needles. Work even in stockinette for another 3cm [1.25in].

Bind off loosely on 3.5mm (US 4) [UK 9 or 10] needles. With tapestry needle, sew the hem down on the inside.

Right Leg
Pick up and k5 (6) 7 (7) 8 (9) sts from the centre of the sts cast on for the left leg crotch, place the right leg sts back on the needle and k them as a continuation of the picked up sts, then pick up and k the 4 (5) 6 (6) 7 (8) remaining sts from the left leg crotch. Place marker and join in a rnd.

Work the right leg the same way as the left leg.

Finishing
Sew all ends to the p side of work. If there is a little hole at the join between the legs, this can be closed with a st or two on the p side.

If you ended the legs with ribbing, block the ribbing after washing to make the ribbed section the same width as the leg itself.

A rolled-collar sweater with twisted ribbing and a waves pattern

Wave Sweater

Sizes XS (S-M) L-XL (XXL)

Measurements
Chest: 105 (122) 140 (155)cm
[41.25 (48) 55 (61)in]
Length:
62 (64) 66 (67)cm
[24.5 (25.25) 26 (26.5)in]
Sleeve length (at underarm):
47 (47) 47 (47)cm
[18.5 (18.5) 18.5 (18.5)in]

Needles
Circular needle 4mm (US 6) [UK 8], 60cm [24in]
Circular needle 4.5mm (US 7) [UK 7], 80cm [32in]
If not using Magic Loop technique, use double-pointed (dp) needles in the same sizes for short rnds.
Tapestry needle for finishing.

Knitting Gauge/Tension
16 sts x 20 rows on 4.5mm (US 7) [UK 7] needles in charted pattern = 10 × 10cm (4 × 4 in)

Yarns
Colour A
1 strand Rauma Garn's Vams
Colour 71 (Light Lilac):
400 (450) 500 (550)g
Colour B
1 strand Permin's Bella
Colour 883261 (Lime):
200 (250) 250 (300)g

Info
Sweater is knitted from the top down.

Colour pattern knitting is also called Fair Isle. If you usually carry the yarn in your left hand, work with both colours over your left index finger always in the same order. The colour closest to you (and the needle) will dominate visually, the other, usually the lighter colour, will recede somewhat. There is no twisting involved and the yarn not in use will run straight across the purl side. Be careful not to pull either yarn tight when changing colours. If you carry the yarns in your right hand, always bring the dominant colour from beneath the other and the secondary colour *over* the dominant. If you are comfortable with both styles of knitting, you can pick the dominant (darker) color from your left index and carry the secondary color on your right index to accomplish the same effect.

Neck
Cast on 88 (88) 100 (100) sts with Colour A on 4mm (US 6) [UK 8] needles with Italian cast-on. Join into a rnd and place marker (rnd marker).

Work 2 rnds double-knit:
Rnd 1. *K1 through back loop (tw k1), sl 1 p-wise with yarn in front of work. Rep from * to end of rnd.
Rnd 2. *Sl 1 p-wise with yarn behind work, p1. Rep from * to end of rnd.

Next rnd. *K1 through back loop, p1. Rep from * to end of rnd.
Work even in twisted ribbing (tw rib) as set by last rnd until ribbing is 10cm [4in] long.

Change to 4.5mm (US 7) [UK 7] needles. Work 1 more rnd of tw rib while placing 8 more st markers to indicate raglan inc points. (They should look different from the turn marker and the rnd marker.): K24 (24) 28 (28) sts (back), place marker, tw rib 2 sts, place marker, k16 (16) 18 (18) sts (rt sleeve) place marker, tw rib 2 sts, place marker, k12 (12) 14 (14) sts (1st half of front), place a turn marker, k12 (12) 14 (14) (2nd half of front), place turn marker, work 2 sts tw rib, place marker, k16 (16) 18 (18) sts (left sleeve), place marker, work 2 sts tw rib. The rnd marker is now between the back and the left sleeve.

Raglan Shoulders
Now both increase for the raglan and work short rows for back neckline/shoulders as follows:
*Make 1 left, k to marker, make 1 rt, sl marker, k2, sl marker, make 1 left, k to marker, make 1 rt, sl marker, make 1 left, k to 8 sts before turn marker, turn.

P to beg of rnd, sl marker, p2,
sl marker, p-make 1 rt,
p to marker, p-make 1 left,
sl marker, p2, sl marker, p-make 1 rt, p
to 8 sts before turn marker, turn.
K back to beg of rnd.*

Rep from * to * twice more but turn first at 6 sts, then at 4 sts before turn marker on both k and p sides. This brings the turns closer and closer to the middle of the front piece. After these 4 short rows, remove the turn markers. Total 112 (112) 124 (124) sts.

Now k 1 rnd with raglan incs:
Make 1 left, *k to marker, make 1 rt, sl marker, k2, sl marker, make 1 left. Rep from * to another 3 times, then k to marker, make 1 rt, sl marker, k2.
Total 120 (120) 132 (132) sts.

The sts are divided like this:
32 (32) 36 (36) sts each for front and back sections;
24 (24) 26 (26) sts for each sleeve, including 8 raglan sts (the 2-st furrows between the incs). You have now made 4 raglan inc rnds.

Start pattern following the chart from lower right at the point indicated for each sweater part. Continue making raglan incs on every other rnd as before.

Always work the 2 raglan sts between sweater parts with Colour A. Work the actual raglan incs in whichever colour fits best with the pattern. Be careful to follow the chart as you gradually add new sts.

Rep until you've worked 23 (25) 27 (29) rnds with raglan incs (including the first 4 raglan incs on the short rows).
Total 272 (288) 316 (332) sts.

Now you're reaching the underarm: Make raglan incs every rnd, but ONLY on the edges of the front and back sections, a total 2 (7) 10 (14) times = 280 (330) 356 (392) sts. The sts are now distributed like this: 74 (88) 102 (114) sts for each front and back , 62 (66) 72 (76) sts for each sleeve and 8 raglan sts.

Now divide the work into body and sleeves, beginning and ending each section with 1 raglan st and removing raglan markers as you go:

K75 (89) 103 (115) back sts.
Place 64 (68) 74 (78) sleeve sts on a holder. Cast on 8 (8) 8 (10) sts with both colours for underarm.

K76 (90) 104 (116) front sts.
Place 64 (68) 74 (78) sleeve sts on a holder and cast on 4 (4) 4 (5) sts with both colours, place marker (new beg of rnd), cast on 4(4) 4 (5) more sts with both colours for underarm, and k1 final raglan divider st.
Total 168 (196) 224 (252) sts for body and 64 (68) 74 (78) sts on holders for each sleeve.

Body
Work even in charted pattern until you've completed 3 vertical repeats.
K2 rnds with Colour A, and in the 2nd rnd, inc 14 (16) 20 (20) sts evenly space across rnd by make 1 rt.
Total 182 (212) 244 (268) sts.

Change to 4mm (US 6) [UK 8] needles. Work 7cm [2.75in] in tw ribbing as for neck. Work 2 rnds double-knit as on the neck cast-on and end with Italian bind-off.

Sleeves
Replace one set of sleeve sts back on 4.5mm (US 7) [UK 7] needles, pick up and k the 4 sts from one side of the cast-on underarm sts with Colour A, k the sleeve sts on the needle, pick up and k the 4 sts on other side of the cast-on underarm sts, join into a rnd and place marker. Total 72 (76) 82 (88) sts.

Now work around in stockinette and charted pattern.
K the 2 sts on either side of marker in Colour A in every rnd.

Dec every 9th (8th) 7th (5th) rnd 8 (10) 11 (13) times:
K2tog. k pattern until 2 sts remain, tw k2tog.
Total 56 (56) 60 (62) sts.

Continue in pattern until chart has repeated 3 times from the top of the shoulder or until the sleeve measures 40 (40) 40 (39)cm [15.75 (15.75) 15.75 (15.25)in], starting at the underarm.
K 1 rnd with Colour A.

Change to 4mm (US 6) [UK 8] needles and work 7cm [2.75in] in tw rib.
Work 2 rnds tw double-knit as on the collar and end with Italian bind off.

Make the second sleeve the same way.

Finishing
With tapestry needle, work in all loose ends and wash sweater following yarn manufacturer's instructions. Spread on dry, absorbant surface and block the sweater as it dries.

Chart

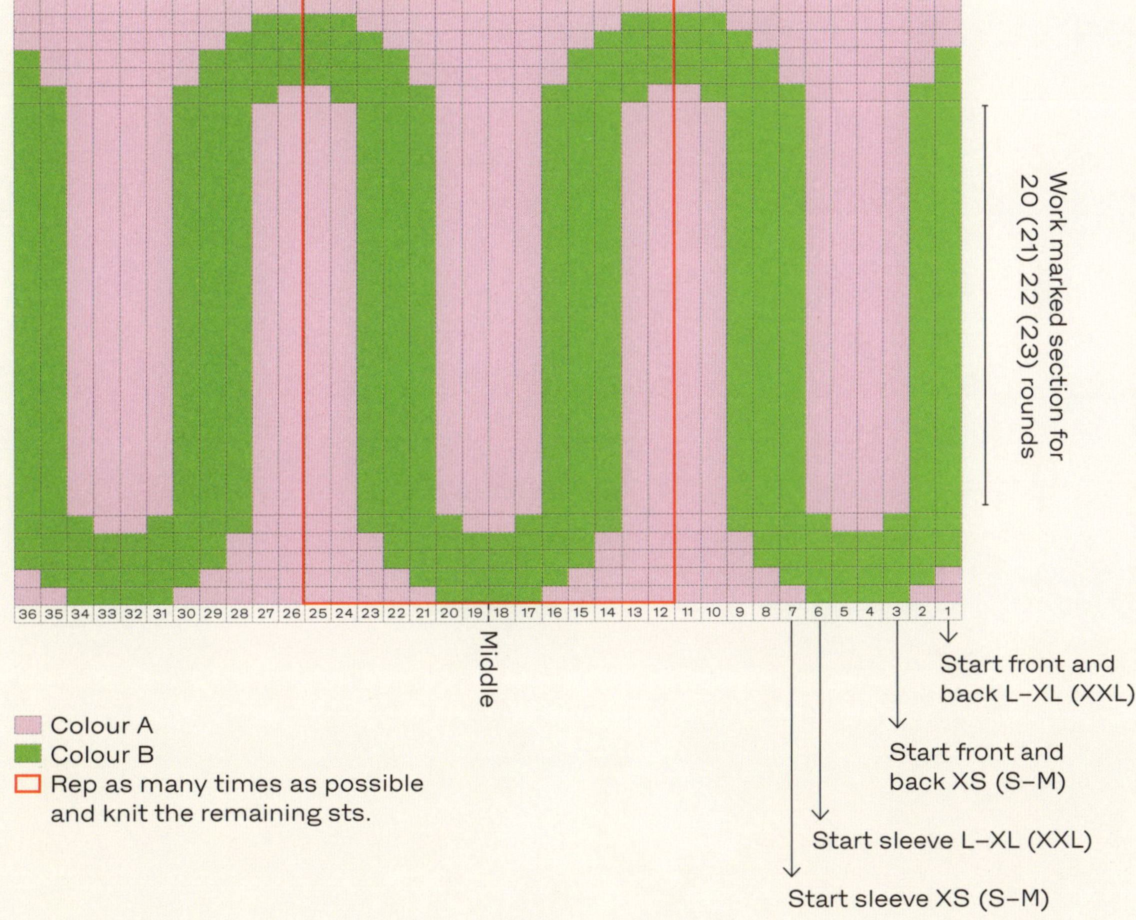

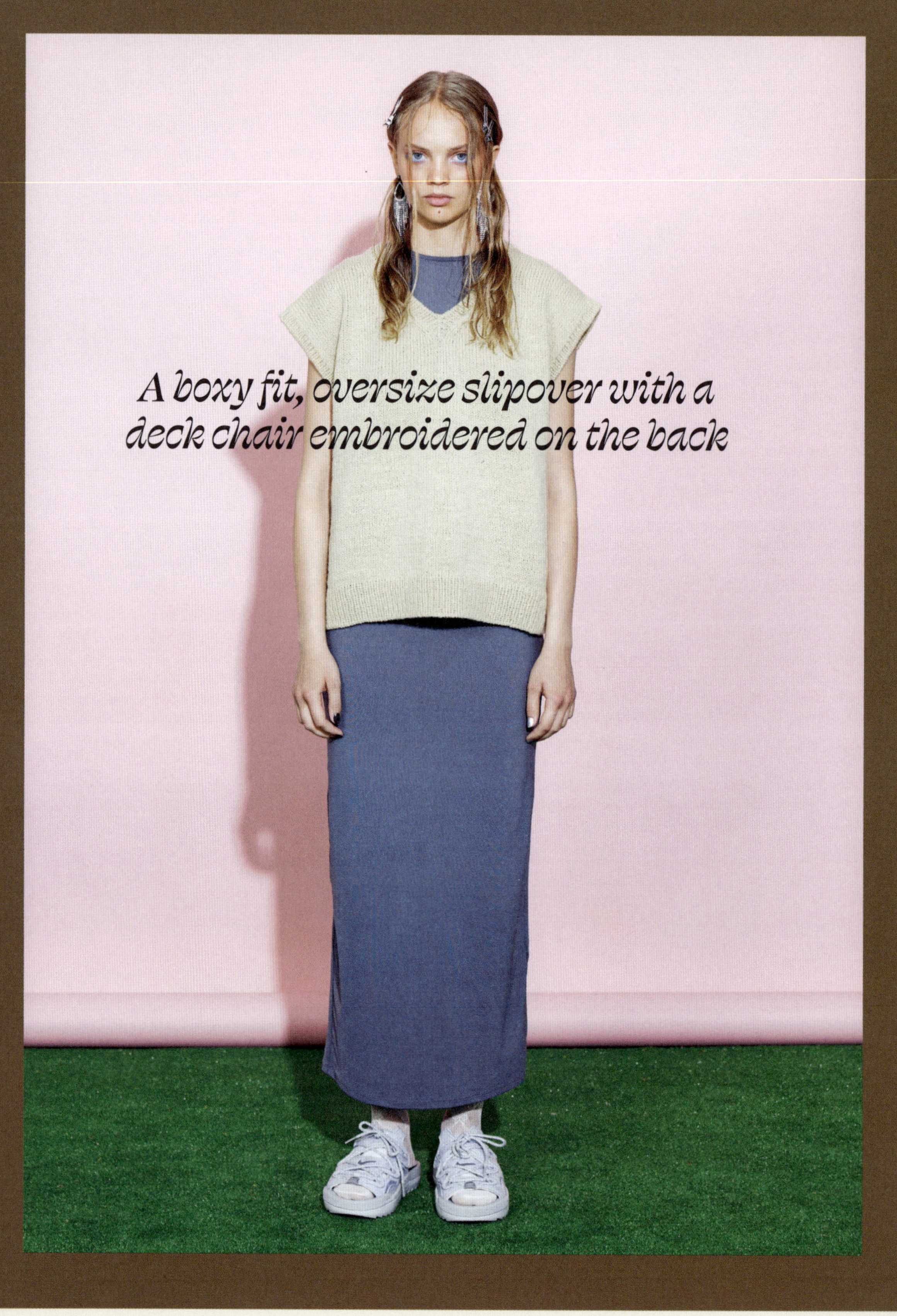

A boxy fit, oversize slipover with a deck chair embroidered on the back

Bianca Slipover

Sizes
XS (S) M (L) XL (XXL)

Measurements
Chest: 102 (107) 118 (121) 135 (141)cm
[40 (42) 46.5 (47.5) 53 (55.5)in]
Length: 62 (64) 64 (65) 66 (67)cm
[24.5 (25.25) 25.25 (25.5) 26in]

Needles
Circular needle 3mm (US 2.5) [UK 11], 60cm [24in]
Circular needle 3.5mm (US 4) [UK 9 or 10], 80cm [32in]
If not using Magic Loop technique, use double-pointed (dp) needles in the same sizes for shorter rnds.
Tapestry needle for embroidery and finishing

Knitting Gauge/Tension
21 sts x 32 rows on 3.5mm (US 4) [UK 9 or 10] needles in stockinette = 10 × 10cm (4 × 4in)

Garn
Rauma Garn's Fivel
Colour 08 (Light straw):
350 (400) 400 (450) 450 (500)g

For embroidery:
Filcolana's Arwetta Classic, 2 strands held together with Filcolana's Tilia, 1 strand

Colour A
Arwetta Classic, Colour 101 (Natural White)
Arwetta Classic, Colour 318 (Ballerina)
Tilia, Colour 101 (Natural White)
Colour B
Arwetta Classic, Colour 318 (Ballerina)
Tilia, Colour 321 (Sakura)
Alternate Colour B
Arwetta Classic, Colour 371 (Hibiscus)
Tilia Colour 322 (Begonia Pink)

Info
The slipover is worked from the top down.

The deck chair on the back is embroidered afterwards with duplicate st.

Back Right Shoulder
Cast 32 (32) 36 (36) 40 (40) sts on 3.5mm (US 4) [UK 9 or 10] needles.
Next row. K1, p until 1 st remains, k1.

Now work short rows to shape the right shoulder, as follows:
K8 (8) 9 (9) 10 (10) sts, turn.
P until 1 st remains, k1.
K14 (14) 16 (16) 18 (18), turn,
p until 1 st remains, k1.
K20 (20) 23 (23) 26 (26), turn,
p until 1 st remains, k1.
K26 (26) 30 (30) 34 (34), turn,
p until 1 st remains in row, k1.
Break yarn and put sts on a holder.

Back Left Shoulder
Cast on 32 (32) 36 (36) 40 (40) sts on 3.5mm (US 4) [UK 9 or 10] needles.

Now work short rows to shape the left shoulder, as follows:
K1, p 7 (7) 8 (8) 9 (9), turn,
k to end of row.
K1, p 13 (13) 15 (15) 17 (17), turn,
k to end of row.
K1, p 19 (19) 22 (22) 25 (25), turn,
k to end of row.
K1, p 25 (25) 29 (29) 33 (33), turn,
k to end of row.
K1, p until 1 st remains, k1.

Now join left and right back pieces:
K the sts on the needle, cast on 33 (35) 35 (37) 37 (39) sts, place the right back section on the needle and k them.
Total 97 (99) 107 (109) 117 (119) sts.

Now work back and forth in stockinette, with a k st as the first and last st of every row until the back is 24cm [9.5in], measured from the highest point of the shoulder. End with a p row.

Now increase to shape the armholes, as follows:
Row 1. (Inc) K4, make 1 left, k until 4 sts remain, make 1 rt, k4.
Row 2. K1, p until 1 st remains, k1.

Work Rows 1–2 a total 6 (7) 9 (10) 13 (15) times.
Break yarn and place sts on a holder.
Total 109 (113) 125 (129) 143 (149) sts.

Left Front Shoulder
With 3.5mm (US 4) [UK 9 or 10] needles, pick up and k32 (32) 36 (36) 40 (40) sts along the k side top edge of the left back shoulder.

Now work 5cm [2in] back and forth in stockinette, with the first and last st in every row as a k st. End with a p row.

Now inc to shape the V-neck:
Row 1. (Inc) K4, make 1 left, k to end of row.
Row 2. K1, p until 1 st remains, k1.

Work Rows 1–2 a total 17 (18) 18 (19) 19 (20) times. Break yarn and place sts on a holder.
Total 49 (50) 54 (55) 59 (60) sts.

Right Front Shoulder
With 3.5mm (US 4) [UK 9 or 10] needles pick up and k32 (32) 36 (36) 40 (40) sts from the k side of the right back shoulder.

Work 5cm [2in] back and forth in stockinette with a k st for the first and last st of every row.

Now inc to shape the V-neck as follows:
Row 1. (Inc) K until 4 sts remain, make 1 rt, k to end of row.
Row 2. K1, then p until 1 st remains, k1.

Work Rows 1–2 a total 17 (18) 18 (19) 19 (20) times.
Total 49 (50) 54 (55) 59 (60) sts.

Join the front pieces as follows:
K the sts on the needle until 1 st remains, put the left front piece back on the needle, k the last st from the rt front piece with the first st of the left front piece, k the sts of the left front.
Total 97 (99) 107 (109) 117 (119) sts.

Now work back and forth in stockinette, with a k st starting and ending every row, until the front measures 24cm [9.5in] from the longest point of the shoulder.
End with a p row.

Now increase to shape the armhole in the same way as on the back.
Total 109 (113) 125 (129) 143 (149) sts.

Body
Now join the front and the back sections at the base of the armholes.
K across the row until 1 st remains. Place the back sts on the needle. Taking the last front st and the first back st, tw k2tog (through their back loops)
k across back until 1 st remains, and take the front first st and the back last st, tw k2tog.
Place marker (beg/end of rnd) and join in a rnd.
Total 216 (224) 248 (256) 284 (296) sts.

K even down in stockinette until the whole slipover measures 54 (55) 56 (57) 58 (59)cm [21.25 (21.75) 22 (22.5) 22.75 (23.25)in], measured down from the top of the shoulder.

Change to 3mm (US 2.5) [UK 11] needles and k 1 rnd, increasing 20 (20) 22 (22) 24 (24) sts, evenly distributed around.
Work 7.5cm [3in] in k1, p1 ribbing.

Work 2 rnds double-knit as follows:
Rnd 1. *K1, sl 1 p-wise with yarn in front. Rep from * to end of rnd.
Rnd 2. *Sl 1 p-wise with yarn behind work, p1. Rep from * to end of rnd.
End with Italian bind-off.

Neck
On 3mm (US 2.5) [UK 11] needles, start at the left shoulder 'seam' and pick up and k50 (54) 55 (58) 60 (60) sts along the left neckline, skipping every 6th st; pick up and k1 st at the bottom of the V and mark it ('marked st'); pick up and k49 (53) 55 (57) 59 (59) sts along the right neckline neckline skipping every 6th st. Finally, pick up and k33 (36) 36 (38) 38 (40) sts along the back neckline, picking up 1 st for every st cast-on st. Place a marker and join in a rnd.

Now dec to shape the V-neck:
Work k1, p1 ribbing to 1 st before the marked st, sl 2 sts off together as if to k2tog, k1, and pass the 2 slipped sts over the k st together. Work k1, p1 ribbing to end of rnd.

Rep * to * a total 6 times, working k over k and p over p at the decs at bottom of the V.

Work 2 rnds double-knit as on body.

End with Italian bind-off.

Left Armhole Ribbing
On 3mm (US 2.5) [UK 11] needles needles, start at the top at the shoulder seam, pick up and k51 (53) 57 (61) 61 (65) sts along the front of the armhole, skipping about every 6th st. Pick up and k1 st at the bottom of the armhole join and mark it (marked stitch), pick up and k60 (62) 64 (66) 66 (70) sts up along the opposite side. Place a marker and join as a rnd.

From this point, k the ribbing in the same way as the neckline ribbing, but rib only 4 rnds before working double-knit for 2 rnds. End with Italian bind-off.

Right Armhole Ribbing
On 3mm (US 2.5) [UK 11] needles, start at the top of the shoulder 'seam' pick up and k60 (62) 64 (66) 66 (70) down along the armhole of the front piece, skipping about every 6th st. Pick up 1 st at the bottom of the underarm join and mark it (the marker st), then pick up and k51 (53) 57 (61) 61 (65) sts along the opposite side. Place a marker (rnd marker) and join into a rnd.

Work the ribbing and double-knit the same way as the the left armhole.

End with Italian bind-off.

Finishing
Sew all tails into the wrong side.

Embroidery
Centre the charted pattern on the back of the slipover and mark the centerline on the chart with a pencil and with a thread on the center line of the slipover back.

On the sweater, count carefully out from the center to start in the right place, at the lower right corner of the chart. Use a tapestry needle to embroider in duplicate st, following the path of each knit st.

Hilda Sweater → 84

A chunky
faux-fur hat

Fat Fur Hat

Sizes
Small (Large)

Measurements
Circumference: 53.5–58 (59–64)cm
[21–22.75 (23–25)in]

Needles
Circular needle 6mm (US 10)
[UK 4], 40–60cm [16–24in]
If not using Magic Loop technique, use double-pointed needles in the same size during decreasing at the crown.
Tapestry needle for finishing.

Knitting Gauge/Tension
12 sts x 18 rows on 6mm (US 10)
[UK 4] needles in stockinette with 2 strands held together = 10 × 10cm (4 × 4in)

Yarn
Permin's Bella
Colour 883258 Pink:
200 (200)g

Other Equipment
Mohair brush

Info
The Fat Fur Hat is knitted as a long, closed tube with decreases at both ends. When completed, the hat is tucked into itself and the edge is turned up.

It is knitted in a long-haired mohair yarn, which is later brushed up with a mohair brush so that the fibres lengthen and seem like fur.

To attain the furry look, a yarn with a long fibre – mohair, alpaca or angora – is recommended.

Hat
Cast on 60 (64) sts loosely on 6mm (US 10) [UK 4] needles with the yarn doubled.

Join in a rnd and place a marker for beg of rnd. Work even in stockinette until work measures 57 (59)cm [22.5 (23.25)in].

Work 1 more rnd, placing 3 more markers:
K 15 (16), place marker,
K 15 (16), place marker,
K 15 (16), place marker, k to end of rnd.

Now decrease:
*K2tog, k to 3 sts before marker, k2tog left, k1. Rep from * another 3 times.
Work last rnd a total 6 times.
Total 12 (16) sts.

Work 1 rnd of k2tog around, removing markers as you work.
Total 6 (8) sts.

Break yarn with a long tail, draw tail through remaining sts once, then again, pull up tight and sew end into reverse side.

Now the other end of the tube needs to be closed with decs. This end will be the inside of the hat.

With 6mm (US 10) [UK 4] needles pick up and k60 (64) sts from the cast on sts, again with doubled yarn. Start at the beg of the rnd. Pick up the sts from the link between the cast-on sts.

K 1 rnd.
Now dec in exactly the way you decreased on the other end of the tube.

Finishing
Work all ends into the fabric using duplicate st. Wash the hat following yarn manufacturer's instructions. Lay it flat to dry.

Brush up the fibres with the mohair brush lengthwise on the hat, from the end bound-off last toward the first bound off end. Take small sections at a time.

Now fold the hat into itself, so that the end bound-off last is tucked completely into the other end. Turn the (new) edge of the hat up so that the new cuff measures about 14–15cm [5.5 (6)in].

A chunky faux-fur boa

Fat Fur Boa

Length 180cm [71in] (approx 6 feet)

Needles
Circular needle 6mm (US 10) [UK 4], 40-60cm [16–24in]
If not using Magic Loop technique use double-pointed needles in the same size.
Tapestry needle for finishing.

Knitting Gauge/Tension
12 sts x 18 rows on 6mm (US 10) [UK 4] needles in stockinette with 2 strands held together = 10 × 10cm (4 × 4 in)

Other Equipment.
A mohair brush

Yarn
Permin's Bella
Colour 883258 Pink: 150g

Info
The Fat Fur Boa is knitted in a long, closed tube, increasing at the beginning and decreasing at the end.

The boa is knitted in a long fibre mohair yarn, which is brushed up with a mohair brush at the end, so the fibres become long and fur-like. To get the furry look, a yarn with a long fibre is recommended, like mohair, alpaca or angora.

Boa
Cast on 8 sts on 6mm (US 10) [UK 4] needles with two strands held together. Join in a rnd and place a marker.

Now inc:
Next rnd. *K2, make 1 rt. Rep from * to end of rnd.
Next rnd. *K3, make 1 rt. Rep from * to end of rnd.
Continue this pattern, increasing the number of sts before/between incs each rnd until there are a total 28 sts, and you have worked a total 5 inc rnds.

K even in stockinette until the boa measures 180cm [71in] (approx 6 feet)
Now dec to shape the second end:
Next rnd. *K5, k2tog. Rep from * to end of rnd.
Next rnd. *K4, k2tog. Rep from * to end of rnd.

Continue this pattern, knitting 1 st less before/between decs each rnd until 8 sts remain and you have made a total 5 dec rnds.

Break yarn with a long tail and with tapestry needle, draw tail through remaining sts once, pull up firmly, draw tail through again, pull up once more and sew tail into fabric.

Finishing
Wash the boa according to yarn manufacturer's instructions.

Lay the boa flat to dry, then, with the mohair brush, brush up the fibres lengthwise, from the centre outward. Work small sections at a time.

A super-simple, mega-chunky sweater

Rose Sweater

Sizes
XS (S) M (L) XL (XXL)

Measurements
Chest: 102 (106) 111 (120) 128 (133)cm
[40 (41.75) 43.75 (47.25) 50.5 (52.5)in]
Length: 51 (52) 53 (54) 55 (56)cm
[20 (20.5) 21 (20.25) 20.75 (22)in]
Sleeve Length: 48 (48) 48 (48) 48 (48)cm
[19 (19) 19 (19) 19 (19)in]

Needles
Circular needle 9mm (US 11) [UK 00], 80cm [32in].
If not using Magic Loop technique use double-pointed needles in the same size for neckline and sleeves.
Large-eyed yarn needle for finishing.

Knitting Gauge/Tension
9 sts x 24 rows on 9mm (US 11) [UK 00] needles with the two yarns held together = 10 × 10cm (4 × 4in)

Yarns
Uld La La's Chunky:
750 (800) 850 (900) 950g

Held together with

Strikkefeber's Fluffy Mohair
Colour: Elfenben FM073 Ivory
300 (300) 300 (350) 400g

Info
Knitted from the top down

The entire sweater is knitted with the two yarns held together.

Neck
Cast on 38 (38) 38 (38) 42 (42) sts on 9mm (US 11) [UK 00] needles. Join ends to make a rnd and place a beg/end of rnd marker.

K7 rnds.

K1 more rnd and divide sts into groups with 4 markers, including a turn marker (for short rows):
K12 (12) 12 (12) 14 (14) sts (back), place marker;
k7 (7) 7 (7) 7 (7) sts (right sleeve), place marker;
k6 (6) 6 (6) 7 (7) (right front), place turn marker;
k6 (6) 6 (6) 7 (7) (left front), place marker;
k to rnd marker (left sleeve).

The rnd marker lies between the back and the left sleeve. Use a different type or colour marker for the beg/end of rnd marker, so you can readily see the difference.

Raglan
Knit short rows now to shape the neckline, while starting the raglan shoulder incs.
For the short rows, use the German Short Rows method as follows:
K1, make 1 left, *k to 1 st before marker, make 1 rt, k2, make 1 left. Rep from * once more, k to 1 st before turn-marker, turn.
P to rnd marker.

P1, make 1 rt, p to 1 st before marker, p-make 1 rt, p2, p-make 1 left, p to 1 st before turn marker, turn.
K to rnd marker.

K1, make 1 left, *k to 1 st before marker, make 1 rt, k2, make 1 left. Rep from * once more, k to 3 sts before turn marker, turn.
P to rnd marker.

P1, p-make 1 rt, p to 1 st before marker, p-make 1 left, p2, p-make 1 rt, p to 3 sts before turn marker, turn.
K to rnd marker.

There are now 2 sets of raglan inc rows.
Total 54 (54) 54 (54) 58 (58) sts.

From this point, work in rnds again.

Continue to inc for raglan as follows:
Rnd 1. K1, make 1 left, *k until 1 sts before marker, make 1 rt, k2, make 1 left.
Repeat from * another 3 times (total 4), then k to 1 st before marker, make 1 rt, k1.
Rnd 2. K to end of rnd.
Work Rnds 1–2 a total 12 (13) 14 (15) 16 (17) times.

You've now worked 14 (15) 16 (17) 18 (19) inc rnds = 150 (158) 166 (174) 186 (194) sts, divided into sections: 40 (42) 44 (46) 50 (52) sts each for front and back and 35 (37) 39 (41) 43 (45) sts for each sleeve.

Body

Now separate the work into body and sleeves. Remove markers as you go.
K across back sts, set the right sleeve sts on a holder, cast on 6 (6) 6 (8) 8 (8) sts (underarm), k the sts for the front, place the left sleeve sts on a holder and cast on 6 (6) 6 (8) 8 (8) sts (underarm), placing a marker after the 3rd (3rd) 3rd (4) 4th (4th) underarm st as a new rnd marker).
Total 92 (96) 100 (108) 116 (120) sts.

Continue in stockinette until work is 44 (45) 46 (47) 48 (49)cm [17.25 (17.75) 18 (18.5) 19 (19.25)in] long, measured from the top of the back neckband, or 7cm [2.75in] short of your desired length.

K 1 rnd and dec 12 (12) 14 (14) 16 (16) sts evenly across rnd by k2tog,
K for 7cm [2.75in] in stockinette.
Bind off in purl.

Sleeves.

Place one set of sleeve sts back on 9mm (US 11) [UK 00] needles.
Pick up and k6 (6) 6 (8) 8 (8) sts from the sts cast on for the underarm and place a marker for the beg/end of rnd after the 3rd (3rd) 3rd (4th) 4th (4th) st.
Total 41 (43) 45 (49) 51 (53) sts.

Continue in stockinette and dec every 7th (7th) 6th (5th) 5th (4th) rnd 6 (6) 7 (9) 9 (10) times as follows: K1, k2tog 2, k until 3 sts remain, k2tog left, k1.
Total 29 (31) 31 (31) 33 (33) sts after all decs have been worked.

From this point, k even in stockinette until the sleeve is 41cm [16.25in] long, measured along the underarm, or 7cm [2.75in] short of your desired length.

K 1 rnd and dec 8 (9) 8 (8) 11 (12) sts evenly across rnd by k2tog.
K for 7cm [2.75in] in stockinette.
Bind off in purl.

Make the other sleeve using the same directions.

Finishing

Sew all loose ends into back of work.

A raglan polo sweater with crocheted lace on the collar

Lace Polo

Sizes
XS (S) M (L) XL (XXL)

Measurements
Chest: 93 (99) 109 (116) 122 (130)cm
[36.75 (39) 43 (45.75) 48 (51)in]
Length: 53 (55) 56 (57) 58 (59)cm
[21 (21.75) 22 (22.5) 22.75 (23.25)in]
Sleeve Length: 41 (41) 41 (41) 41 (41)cm
[16 (16) 16 (16) 16 (16)in]

Needles
Circular needle 3mm (US 2.5) [UK 11], 60cm [24in]
Circular needle 3.5mm (US 4) [UK 9 or 10], 80cm [32in]
If not using Magic Loop technique, use double-pointed needles in the same size for neckline and sleeves.
Tapestry needle for finishing.
Crochet hook 3mm (US D) [UK 11]

Knitting Gauge/Tension
21 sts x 29 rows on 3.5mm (US 4) [UK 9 or 10] needles with Colour A = 10 × 10cm (4 × 4in)

Yarns
Colour A
Permin's Bella
Green version: 883282(Light Green)
Pink version: 883264 (Delicate Rose)
250 (300) 300 (350) 350 (400)g
Colour B
Filcolana's Arwetta Classic
Green version: 250 (Disco Green)
Pink version: 101 (Natural White)
50 (50) 50 (50) 50 (50)g

Info
The whole sweater is worked in Colour A, except the lacy edge of the collar, which is crocheted with Colour B. Sweater is worked from the top down.

When working in rows, a selvage- or edge-stitch is worked by slipping the first st purlwise with the yarn in front of the needle. In the next row, on the purl side, the same st is knitted.

Collar
Cast on 101 (101) 105 (105) 105 (105) sts somewhat loosely on size UK 9 or 10 (US 4) [3.5mm] needles with Colour A.
Row 1. Sl 1 p-wise, p until 1 st remains, k1.
Row 2. Sl 1 p-wise, k2tog, k until 3 sts remain, k2tog left, k1.

Work Rows 1–2 a total 14 times = 73 (73) 77 (77) 77 (77) sts.

The next row is k and the p side of the collar now becomes the sweater's k side. Place markers as follows:
K12 (12) 13 (13) 13 (13), place marker (one part of the front) K12, place marker (left sleeve and beg of rnd marker). K24 (24) 26 (26) 26 (26), place marker (back), K12, place marker(right sleeve).

K until 1 st remains in the row (2nd part of front), k the last st with the first st of the row to form a round, place marker (turn marker). K to beg of rnd marker. Total 72 (72) 76 (76) 76 (76) sts

The beg-of-rnd marker lies between the back and the left sleeve.
Ideally use a different type/ colour of marker, so you can see the difference between turn, raglan, and rnd markers.

Raglan Shoulders
Now work around in stockinette but first k briefly back and forth on short rows to shape the neckline while you also begin to increase for the raglan shoulders.

For the short rows, we recommend the German Short Rows technique as follows:
K1, make 1 left, *k until 1 st before marker, make 1 rt, k2, make 1 left. Rep from * once more, then k until 10 sts before turn marker, turn.
P back to beg of rnd.
P1, p-make 1 rt, p until 1 st before marker, p-make 1 left, p2, p-make 1 rt, p to 10 sts before turn marker, turn.
K to beg of rnd.

Work these 2 short rows another 2 times but move your turning point 2 sts closer to the turn marker each time. The turns are thus moved closer and closer to the centre of the front.

There are now 4 sets of raglan incs. From here on, work circularly in rnds again. Total 104 (104) 108 (108) 108 (108) sts.

Continue to make raglan incs:
Rnd 1. (Inc) K1, make 1 left, *k to 1 st before marker, make 1 rt, k2, make 1 left. Rep from * twice more, k to 1 st before marker, make 1 rt, k1.
Rnd 2. K to end of rnd.

Work Rows 1–2 a total of 23 (24) 25 (26) 27 (28) times.

Now inc in every rnd, so only rep Rnd 1.

Work Rnd 1 a total 4 (6) 8 (11) 13 (16) times. You have now worked 31 (34) 37 (41) 44 (48) raglan rnds. Total 320 (344) 356 (391) 428 (460) sts, divided like this: 86 (92) 100 (108) 114 (122) sts each for front and back sections and 74 (80) 86 (94) 100 (108) sts for each sleeve.

Body
Divide the sts into body and sleeves. Remove markers as you go. K the back sts, place the sts for the right sleeve on a holder. Cast on 12 (12) 14 (14) 14 (14) sts (right underarm), k across the front section, place the left sleeve sts on a holder, cast on 6 (6) 7 (7) 7 (7) sts (left underarm) and place a new beg-of-rnd marker, cast on 6 (6) 7 (7) 7 (7) more sts for the rest of the left underarm. Total 196 (208) 228 (244) 256 (272) sts for the body.

Continue even in stockinette until the body is 45 (46) 47 (48) 49 (50)cm [17.75 (18) 18.5 (19) 19.25 (19.75)in] long, measured from back of neck (below the collar) or 8cm [3.25in] shorter than your desired length.

Change to 3mm (US 2.5) [UK 11] needles and work 8cm [3.25in] in k1, p1 ribbing. Bind off loosely in ribbing.

Sleeves
The two sleeves are worked identically. Place one set of sleeve sts on 3.5mm (US 4) [UK 9 or 10] needles.
Pick up and k12 (12) 14 (14) 14 (14) sts from those sts cast on at the underarm and place a marker in the middle of these (rnd marker).
Total 86 (92) 100 (108) 114 (122) sts.

Continue in stockinette and dec every 6th (6th) 5th (5th) 4th (4th) rnd 7 (17) 21 (21) 21 (26) times:
K1, k2tog, k until 3 sts remain in rnd, k2tog left, k1.
Total 52 (58) 58 (66) 72 (70) sts.

From here, k even in stockinette until sleeve is 36cm [14in] long, measured along the dec line of the sleeve, or until 8cm [3.25in] shorter than desired final length. Change to 3mm (US 2.5) [UK 11] needles and work 8cm [3.25in] in k1, p1 ribbing.

Bind off loosely in ribbing. Make the 2nd sleeve following these directions.

Lace Edge on Collar
With 3mm (US D) [UK 11] crochet hook and Colour B, crochet the lace edge around the collar. Start at centre front on right side of the collar's outer edge:

Attach yarn to collar by slip st at centre front, *3 chain sts, 1 st into the front loop of the first chain st, skip 2 sts in the knit edge, double crochet (single crochet for US) into the next st. Rep from* the whole way around the outside edge of the collar. You should end with a perfectly repeating series of delicate points along the collar edge.

Finishing
Sew all ends into the purl side of the sweater. Wash it according to yarn manufacturer's instructions. It's important to block the collar before it dries, as otherwise it will curl.

Mega Bibi
Slipover → 54

Yarn

Alpakka Ull from Sandnes
65% Alpaca and 35% wool
100m [109yds] / 50g [1.75oz]

Arwetta Classic from Ficolana
80% Merino wool and 20% nylon
210m {230yds] / 50g [1.75oz]

Bella from Permin
75% kid mohair, 20% wool and 5% polyamid
145m [159yds] / 50g [1.75oz]

Chunky from Uld la la
100% Falklands Merino wool
70m [77yds] / 100g [3.5oz]

Cotton Wool 5 from Gepardgarn
50% organic cotton and 50% Merino wool
100m [109yds] / 50g [1.75oz]

Fivel from Rauma Garn
100% Norwegian wool
100m [109yds] / 50g [1.75oz]

Fluff from HipKnitShop
80% kid mohair, 11% Merino wool and 9% polyamid
100m [109yds] / 50g [1.75oz]

Fluffy Mohair from Strikkefeber
78% Mohair, 13% wool and 9% nylon
100m [109yds] / 50g [1.75oz]

Thick Mohair from Honse x Spektakelstrik
78% kid mohair, 13% Merino wool and 9% nylon
200m [219yds] / 100g [3.5oz]

KOS from Sandnes
62% baby alpaca, 9% wool, 29% nylon
150m [164yds] / 50g [1.75oz]

Le Gros Silk & Mohair from Biches & Bûches
28% mulberry silk and 72% super kid mohair
148m [162yds] / 50g [1.75oz]

Le Petit Silk & Mohair from Biches & Bûches
30% mulberry silk and 70% super kid mohair
212m [232yds]/ 25g

Pernilla from Filcolana
100% wool
175m [191yds] / 50g [1.75oz]

Peruvian Highland Wool from Filcolana
100% wool
100m [109yds] / 50g [1.75oz]

Plum from Rauma Garn
70% super kid mohair and 30% polyamid
250m [273yds] / 25g [approx 1oz]

Saga from Filcolana
100% wool
300m [328 yds]/ 50g [1.75oz]

Tynn Silk Mohair from Sandnes
57% mohair, 28% silk and 15% wool
212m [232yds] / 25g [approx 1oz]

Tilia from Filcolana
70% kid mohair and 30% silk
210m [230yds]/ 25g [approx 1oz]

Vams from Rauma Garn
100% Norwegian wool
100m [109yds] / 50g [1.75oz]

Abbreviations

ctr dbl p dec: centred double purl decrease: Slip 2 sts, one by one, knit-wise to right needle, slip the 2 sts back together onto the left needle by inserting the left needle first into the second to last stitch on the right needle, then into the last. Replace them on the left needle. Purl them and the next st on left needle together.

ctr-dbl-dec: centred double (knit) decrease: sl 2, k1, p2sso to dec 2 sts at once: Slip 2 sts at once from left needle as if to knit, knit 1, pass (the two) slipped sts together over the knit stitch. Object is to have 2 decreases at once, leaning into a central retained stitch.

dec: decrease.

inc: increase

k2tog: knit 2 together, a decrease leaning right.

k: knit, as opposed to purl

k2tog left: k2 sts together: slip 1 st p-wise, replace on left needle, knit 2 together. Leans left.

make 1 left: make 1 inc leaning left: Insert left needle into the strand between sts from the front and k1 st into the back of the loop.

make 1 rt: make 1 k st leaning rt: Insert left needle under the strand between sts from behind and k1 st into that loop.

p: purl

p2tog: purl 2 sts together. Leans left on knit side

p-make 1 rt: make 1 purl inc leaning left: Lift strand between sts onto left needle from behind and p1 st.

p-make 1 left: make 1 purl increase leaning rt: Lift strand between sts onto left needle from in front and p1 st through back.

rep: repeat (what went before).

rnd: round

rs: right side, or knit side, or outside. opposed to **ws** (reverse, purl, or inside).

rt: right (vs. left)

Sl 1 p-wise: selvage stitch or edge-stitch. Slip 1 stitch purlwise with yarn held in front of work with the yarn in front of the needle, to create a smooth non-curling vertical edge.

st, sts: stitch, stitches

tog: together, as 'knit 2 together.'

tw k2tog: twisted knit 2 stitches together: Slip 1 st knit-wise, replace on left needle, knit 2 sts together. Leans right.

tw k: twisted knit stitch. Knit into back of st.

Tw k2tog: twisted knit 2 together. (leans left): Slip 1 st knit-wise, slip 1 more st knit-wise, return them in that position to the left needle, then k2 sts together (k2tog) through the back loop.

tw p: twisted purl, slip 2 sts knit-wise, replace on left needle, purl through back loops.

tw p2tog: twisted purl 2 stitches together: Bring yarn forward, sl 2 sts k-wise onto right needle. Replace together onto left needle. Purl 2 together through back loop. Leans right on knit side.

ws: wrong side, purl side, reverse side, or inside, of work. I used wrong side because there is not much purling on what is usually called the purl side.

yds: yards

yo: yarn over. Lift working yarn over right needle as if to knit, but don't knit. This creates a hole when knitted in the next round or row.

EDITION

Thanks!

Thanks to yarn suppliers Gepard Garn, Rauma Garn, Sandnes Garn, Filcolana, Permin, HipKnitShop, Biches & Bûches, Uld la la, Honse and Galaxy Glow for working with me and for all that luscious yarn.

Thanks to all my hard working test knitters, who have put great effort into every little stitch. Without you, there would have been no book. THANK YOU!

Thanks to my sweet husband and my dear children, who have given hugs and love.

Thank you, Bianca, for knitting, sparring, and keeping the office as neat as a sharp knife.

Thank you, Bitten from Strandparken Camping, for lending us Aalborg's very best camp site.

Thanks to Rikke for texts and dancing breaks.

Thanks to Kirsten and Helmer.

Thanks to Dear Denier for donating tights.

Thank you, Birgitte from Madsine, for discussion and moral support.

Thank you, Vigga, Mari, Aksel, Maria and Anna, for being wonderful models.

Thanks to Hanne and Tommy for lending their camper.

Not least, my thanks to Politikens Forlag, who sent me a letter on a cold December day and made my 2023 much more exciting. Gosh, that was lit!